STUDY GUIDE WITH DISK

for use with

INTRODUCTION TO ACCOUNTING: AN INTEGRATED APPROACH

VOLUME I CHAPTERS 1-13

Penne Ainsworth
Dan Deines
R. David Plumlee
Cathy Xanthaky Larson

Prepared by

Debra K. Kerby
Scott R. Fouch
Both of Truman State University

**Irwin
McGraw-Hill**

Boston, Massachusetts   Burr Ridge, Illinois   Dubuque, Iowa
Madison, Wisconsin   New York, New York   San Francisco, California   St. Louis, Missouri

Irwin/McGraw-Hill

A Division of The McGraw-Hill Companies

Printed in the United States of America.

ISBN 0–256–24348–4

67890 QPD 098

Table of Contents

Chapter 1 Business and Accounting

Learning Objective 1:

Describe the development of accounting and business, the four basic concepts of accounting, and role of risk and reward in business.

Summary

Six eras are discussed in the development of business and accounting. Four basic accounting concepts were developed through these eras. These concepts are: the business entity concept, the going concern concept, the monetary unit concept, and the periodicity concept. The evaluation of risk and reward is important in making business decisions.

Learning Objective 2:

Explain the differences among business industry types and business organizational structures.

Summary

Business industry types include merchandising firms (acquire goods for distribution to consumers), service firms (provide services for consumers), and manufacturing firms (produce products from raw materials for sale to consumers). Business organizational structures include sole proprietorships (one owner), partnerships (two or more owners), and corporations. Sole proprietors and partners place their personal belongings at risk if the business fails. See Exhibit 1-2 for a comparison of the characteristics of ownership structures.

Learning Objective 3:

Define external and internal stakeholders and explain the interest each type of stakeholder has in business in the 1990s.

Summary

External stakeholders are parties outside the organization who have an interest in the organization. They include creditors, governmental units, suppliers, customers, and the general public. Internal stakeholders are parties inside the organization, such as employees and managers.

Outline of Key Concepts

I. The development of business and accounting has been linked through time.

    A. Business is the exchange of goods, services, and money, on an arms-length basis, that results in mutual benefit or profit for both parties involved.

    B. Accountability is responsibility.

        1. Accounting systems provide information to hold businesses accountable for the resources entrusted to them by others.

        2. An accounting system is used to identify, analyze, measure, record, summarize, and communicate relevant economic information to interested parties.

    C. Important eras in the development of business and accounting.

        1. The ancient merchants of Babylonia (2285-2242 B.C.).

            a. Sole proprietorship--a business owned by one person. The owner places his/her personal belongings at risk if the business fails.

            b. Merchandising company--obtains and distributes goods to consumers.

        2. Venture trading (eleventh to thirteenth centuries).

            a. Service firms--provide services for their customers (banking).

            b. Partnership--business owned by two or more individuals. Personal belongings are at risk if the business fails.

        3. Growth beyond the one venture concept and development of two important accounting concepts.

            a. Business entity concept--an accounting system records and summarizes only those economic events that pertain to a particular entity.

            b. Going concern concept--absent information to the contrary, the business will continue into the foreseeable future.

4. Pacioli and the Method of Venice (the evolution of double-entry accounting).

    a.   Double-entry system--a bookkeeping system that records two sides of each economic event. Appropriate numbers are entered into the accounting records twice.

    b.   Luca Pacioli included several chapters on the double-entry accounting system in a mathematics textbook (1494).

    c.   Monetary unit concept--money is the common measurement unit of economic activity.

    d.   Periodicity concept--profits of the business must be determined at regular intervals during the life of the business.

5. Industrial revolution and the advent of the corporation.

    a.   Manufacturing firms--produce products from raw materials for sale to consumers.

    b.   Corporation
        i.   Business entity that is legally separate and distinct from its owners.

        ii.   Limited liability--investors are not personally liable for the debts of the corporation.

6. Standardization of Accounting.

    a.   Sixteenth Amendment to the Constitution established a system of federal income taxes.

    b.   Stock market crash of 1929 led to the Securities and Exchange Acts of 1933 and 1934 which require the disclosure of certain financial information by publicly owned corporations.

II. Generally Accepted Accounting Principles

    A.   Financial Accounting Standards Board (FASB) is a full-time group of professionals.

        1.   Developing accounting standards for reporting to external financial statement users.

        2.   Issue Statements of Financial Accounting Standards (SFAS).

    B.   Generally accepted accounting principles (GAAP) guide acceptable accounting practice.

        1.   Includes the SFASs, the bulletins, opinions, and principles of two previous accounting rule-making bodies (CAP and APB).

            a.   Includes the four basic concepts discussed above.

    C.   Only a certified public accountant (CPA) can attest that a company's financial information has been fairly presented in accordance with GAAP.

III. Business in the 1990s

    A.   People go into business to achieve monetary and personal goals.

    B.   Investing in corporations.

        1.   Share of stock--certificate that represents ownership in the corporation.

        2.   Return on investment (ROI)--profit received on the owner's investment in the corporation.

        3.   Bond--a certificate that represents the debt of the company.

    C.   Factors affecting business performance include swings in the economic cycle, changes in the interest rate, and consumer confidence in the economy.

D. Characteristics of business organizational structure (See Exhibit 1-2).

    1. Sole proprietorship--one owner, limited life, unlimited liability, no business taxation, not a separate legal entity.

    2. Partnership--two or more owners (with mutual agency), limited life, unlimited liability, no business taxation, and not a separate legal entity.

    3. Corporation--one or more shareholders, unlimited life, limited liability, business taxation, a separate legal entity.

        a. Double taxation--profits of the corporation are taxed at the business level and again at the stockholder level if the profits are distributed as dividends.

E. The Stakeholders--those who have an interest in an organization. Who gets priority?

    1. Stockholders--the owners.

    2. External stakeholders--parties outside an organization who have an interest in the organization. Includes creditors, governmental units, suppliers, customers, and the general public.

    3. Internal stakeholders--parties inside an organization who have an interest in the organization. Includes employees and managers.

    4. Which stakeholders get priority?

F. There are five functional areas in business: marketing, human resource management, production and operations, finance, and accounting and information systems.

Problem I

Indicate whether the following statements are either true (T) or false (F).

1. Accounting systems have remained relatively unchanged in the last 100 years.
2. A merchandising company produces products from raw materials for sale to consumers.
3. A stockholder would be considered an internal stakeholder of a company.
4. A limited partner is personally liable for the debts of the partnership.
5. The Financial Accounting Standards Board is responsible for developing accounting standards for external reporting.
6. A business operated as a corporation will be subject to double taxation.
7. Money has always been considered the common measurement unit of an economic activity.
8. The marketing function is responsible for planning and controlling the operations of a business.
9. The marketing function within a business is responsible for reporting results of operations to interested parties.
10. A share of stock is the certificate that represents ownership in a corporation.

Problem II

Indicate the correct answer by circling the appropriate letter.

1. Which of the following is considered a separate legal entity?
   a. partnership
   b. corporation
   c. sole proprietorship
   d. limited partnership

2. Which functional area within a company has the responsibility for determining the wants and needs of its customers?
   a. finance function
   b. marketing function
   c. accounting and information systems function
   d. human resource function
   e. production and operation function

3. Ralph purchased stock for $5,000 and sold it after one year for $5,300. Ralph's return on investment is _____.
   a. 3%
   b. 6%
   c. 10%
   d. 100%

4. Wal-mart would be considered a _____firm.
   a. service
   b. merchandising
   c. manufacturing
   d. none of the above

5. Which functional area would have the responsibility for preparing financial statements used by the owners of a business?
   a. finance function
   b. marketing function
   c. accounting and information systems function
   d. human resource function
   e. production and operation function

6. Katie purchased 100 shares of stock of a utility company for $2,000. At the end of one year, Katie received a cash dividend of $40 on the stock. Katie's return on investment is _____.
   a. 2%
   b. 5%
   c. 10%
   d. 25%

7. Which of the following is not an advantage of a corporation over a partnership?
   a. unlimited life
   b. limited liability
   c. no entity level tax imposed
   d. all of the above are advantages of a corporation

Problem III

The following is a list of important ideas and key concepts from the chapter. To test your knowledge of these terms, match the term with the definition by placing the number in the space provided.

15	Accounting	3	Limited liability
18	Accounting system	9	Monetary unit concept
19	Auditing	23	Partnership
1	Business entity concept	13	Periodicity concept
6	Chief financial officer	22	Return of capital
2	Corporation	12	Return on capital
4	External stakeholder		Reward
5	Financial Accounting Standards Board (FASB)	11	Risk
16	Fiscal year		Sole proprietorship
10	Generally accepted accounting principles (GAAP)	7	Statements of Financial Accounting Standards
21	Going concern concept		
14	Internal auditor		
8	Internal stakeholder		

1. The concept that requires that an accounting system reflect information that records and summarizes only those economic events that pertain to a particular entity

2. A business entity that is legally separate and distinct from its owners

3. The condition that investors are not personally liable for the debts of the business

4. Parties outside an organization who have an interest, or stake, in the organization, such as stockholders, creditors, suppliers, customers and the general public

5. The body responsible for developing accounting standards for reporting to external financial statement users

6. A member of top management to whom the controller, treasurer and internal auditor report

7. The pronouncements of the Financial Accounting Standards Board

8. Parties inside the organization who have an interest, or stake, in the organization, such as employees and management

9. The concept that asserts that money is the common measurement unit of economic activity

10. The Statements of Financial Accounting Standards, bulletins, opinions and principles that direct acceptable accounting practice

11. Sacrifices of an action

12. The return, or profit, generated by a capital investment

13. The concept that requires that the profits of the business be determined at regular intervals throughout the life of the business

14. An individual responsible for developing and implementing the company's system of accounting and administrative controls

15. Responsibility

16. A year-long period that encompasses a natural business cycle and allows a corporation to prepare its required accounting information during its slowest business period

17. A business owned by one person whose personal possessions are at risk

18. A system used to identify, analyze, measure, record, summarize and communicate relevant economic information to interested parties

19. The process of examining a company's financial records by a CPA to ascertain whether they comply with generally accepted accounting principles

20. Benefits of an action

21. The concept that assumes that, absent information to the contrary, the business will continue into the foreseeable future

22. The return of capital invested

23. A business owned by two or more individuals whose respective personal possessions are at risk

Problem IV

Complete the following sentences by filling in the correct response.

1. The _Accounting Information System_ is a system that is used to identify, analyze, measure, record, summarize and communicate relevant economic information to interested parties.

2. The _Business entity_ concept requires that the accounting system keep a business's economic events separate from other economic events of the owners.

3. Absent information to the contrary, the _going concern_ concept assumes that a business entity will continue in existence into the foreseeable future.

4. A company's customer would be considered an _external_ stakeholder.

5. The _Finance_ function is responsible for managing the capital resources of a company.

6. When the SEC requires companies to prepare annual financial statements, it is applying the _Periodicity_ concept.

7. A company that produces microcomputers would be considered a _Manufacturing_ firm.

8. The _Controller_ is a company's chief accounting officer.

9. _Internal_ auditors have responsibility for developing and implementing the company's system of accounting and administrative controls.

10. Employees would be considered _Internal_ stakeholders of a company.

11. A _Bond_ is a certificate that represents the debt of a company.

12. _Mutual agency_ is a situation in which each partner has the power to act for all other partners.

13. Only _Certified Public Accountant_ can attest to the presentation of financial information of a publicly held company.

Solutions for Chapter 1

Problem 1

1.	F	6.	T
2.	F	7.	F
3.	F	8.	F
4.	F	9.	F
5.	F	10.	T

Problem II

1. b
2. b
3. b
4. b
5. c
6. a
7. c

Problem III

15	Accounting	3	Limited liability
18	Accounting system	9	Monetary unit concept
19	Auditing	23	Partnership
1	Business entity concept	13	Periodicity concept
6	Chief financial officer	22	Return of capital
2	Corporation	12	Return on capital
4	External stakeholder	20	Reward
5	Financial Accounting Standards Board (FASB)	11	Risk
16	Fiscal year	17	Sole proprietorship
10	Generally accepted accounting principles (GAAP)	7	Statements of Financial Accounting Standards
21	Going concern concept		
14	Internal auditor		
8	Internal stakeholder		

Problem IV

1. accounting information system
2. business entity
3. going concern
4. external
5. finance
6. periodicity
7. manufacturing
8. controller
9. internal
10. internal
11. bond
12. Mutual agency
13. Certified Public Accountants

Chapter 2   Accounting and Its Role in Business

Learning Objective 1:

Distinguish between external and internal stakeholders and their respective needs for accounting information.

Summary

External stakeholders do not see or participate in the day-to-day operations of the business. They must rely on information provided by the business. External stakeholders use this information to make investment, credit, taxing, regulatory, and other decisions. Internal stakeholders use accounting information to make decisions about future business operations.

Learning Objective 2:

Describe how a company uses accounting subsystems to meet the information needs of external and internal users.

Summary

External stakeholders have diverse accounting information needs. Accounting subsystems generate financial statements, corporate tax returns, regulatory filings, and numerous other documents for use by external stakeholders. Internal users utilize the same financial information that external users can access. In addition, internal users can request special reports to support specific decisions.

Learning Objective 3:

Describe how a company uses the financial accounting subsystem to identify, analyze, measure, and classify accounting events.

Summary

An accounting event possesses three qualities: (1) Specific to an economic entity, (2) Capable of being measured in financial terms, and (3) Two effects that create or change the rights and obligations of the entity. The effect of an accounting event is measured at the cash or cash equivalent cost of the item at the time the event takes place. The effects of accounting events are classified as assets or equities.

Learning Objective 4:

Describe how a company uses the financial accounting subsystem to communicate the results of accounting events to external users.

Summary

The financial accounting subsystem provides information to users through the company's financial statements. The four primary financial statements are (1) the income statement, (2) the statement of owners' equity or the statement of retained earnings, (3) the balance sheet (statement of financial position), and (4) the cash flow statement.

Learning Objective 5:

Describe how a company uses the management accounting subsystem to communicate information to internal users.

Summary

Management accounting information is used for planning and evaluating business decisions, and it is commonly classified as a cost or benefit. Management accounting information may be nonfinancial (such as number of defective units) or financial in nature. The form, content, and time frame of internal reports vary with the user, the decision, and company policy.

Outline of Key Concepts

I. Accounting information needs of external stakeholders.

    A.   External users have need for relevant information--information that is capable of making a difference in the user's decision.

        1.   Information could be in the form of financial statements, corporate tax returns, reports filed with governmental agencies, or other documents.

    B.   Stockholders and creditors need information that indicates whether management is taking undue risks or operating the business inefficiently.

        1.   Users want to know whether they will receive a return of, and a return on, their capital.

        2.   Annual reports are a principal source of information for stockholders and other external users.

            a.   Annual reports contain general information about the company as well as financial statements.

    C.   Governmental units need accounting information.

        1.   Taxation--Corporations pay income taxes to various governmental units, and they have to report information about taxes that are not taxes of the business itself.

        2.   Compliance with government regulation--Public corporations are required to file reports, such as Form 10K, with the Securities Exchange Commission (SEC). Company's may also be required to submit reports about environmental costs.

    D.   Customers and vendors need accounting information.

        1.   These parties are involved in numerous transactions with the business. See Chapter 3 for more details.

II. Accounting information needs of internal stakeholders.

    A.   Internal users need information to plan the business activities required to meet business's goals and to evaluate whether the goals are being met. Information is used to make decisions about future business operations.

B.   Managers will often need accounting information that is not contained in the financial statements.

III. Accounting information system has four subsystems.

    A.   Financial accounting subsystem--designed to communicate information to external users, primarily stockholders and creditors.

    B.   Management accounting subsystem--designed to provide information to internal users.

    C.   Tax accounting subsystem--designed to provide tax and tax-related information to governments.

    D.   Regulatory accounting subsystem--designed to provide required reports to regulatory agencies.

IV. The financial accounting subsystem is used to identify, analyze, measure, and record economic events.

    A.   Economic events occur when you make decisions that affect your wealth.

    B.   Accounting events are economic events with three special qualities.

        1.   Specific to an economic entity--the event has a direct impact on the economic entity for which the accounting records are kept.

        2.   Capable of being measured in financial terms.

        3.   Have two effects that create or change the rights and obligations of the entity.

    C.   Measuring and classifying accounting events.

        1.   The effect of an accounting event is measured at the cash or cash equivalent cost of the item at the time the event takes place.

        2.   The effects of accounting events can be classified as assets or equities.

            a.   Assets--rights to use resources (goods or services) that are expected to result in future economic benefit for the accounting entity. They represent the firm's exclusive rights to control an expected future benefit. Types of assets include accounts receivable, inventory, supplies, and property, plant and equipment. Assets may be classed as current or long-term.

b.   Equities--business obligations to transfer resources to other parties at some future date.

    i.   Liabilities--an obligation to transfer a measurable amount of resources to employees and other providers of goods and services. Examples include salaries payable, accounts payable, and notes payable. Liabilities may be classified as current or long-term.

    ii.   Owners' equity--an obligation to transfer the company's residual resources to the owners of the business in the event the business ceases operations. Contributed capital represents the contributions of the owners to the business. Retained earnings are the accumulated profits of the business.

D.   Duality of the effects of accounting events.

   1.   Every accounting event has two monetarily equal effects on the business entity, which results in the creation of changes in assets and/or equities. This duality results in the following equality:

$$\text{Assets} = \text{Equities}$$

This means that the total assets of the company must always equal the total equities of the company. So for every accounting event, the total change in assets must equal the total change in equities.

   2.   The accounting equation is an expansion of this duality:

$$\text{Assets} = \text{Liabilities} + \text{Owners' Equity}$$

E.   Analyzing and measuring revenue and expense events.

   1.   Revenue--the amount earned by a company for providing goods and services to customers.

    a.   Revenue event-- (1) either an increase in assets or a decrease in liabilities and (2) an increase in owners' equity resulting from the operations of the business.

2. Expense--the amount incurred in an attempt to generate revenue.

    a. Expense event--(1) either a decrease in assets or an increase in liabilities and (2) a decrease in owners' equity resulting from the operations of the business.

3. Net income--the difference between revenue and expense in a certain time period.

V. The financial accounting subsystem communicates relevant information to users through financial statements.

    A. Income Statement--reports to users the revenues, expenses, and resulting net income for a particular period of time. See Exhibit 2.4.

    B. Statement of Owners' Equity--shows the changes that occurred in owners' equity for the period of time covered by the income statement. The statement is a link between the income statement and the balance sheet. See Exhibit 2.5.

        1. The income (loss) on the income statement is presented as an increase (decrease) in owners' equity during the period.

        2. The ending balance in owners' equity is shown on the balance sheet.

    C. Balance Sheet or Statement of Financial Position--shows the assets, liabilities, and owners' equity that exist at the end of the period covered by the income statement. It illustrates the accounting equation. See Exhibit 2.6.

    D. Statement of Cash Flows--shows the business's cash inflows and cash outflows as well as the net change in the business's cash balance for the same time period as the income statement. See Exhibit 2.7. The statement is divided into three sections:

        1. Net cash flows from operating activities.

        2. Net cash flows from investing activities.

        3. Net cash flows from financing activities.

    E. Accounting events are reflected in the financial statements.

        1. See Exhibits 2.8, 2.9, and 2.10 for analysis of an event's effect on the financial statements.

        2. Cash flows from operations do not necessarily equal net income.

VI. The management accounting subsystem is designed to provide relevant information to internal stakeholders.

    A.   Management accounting information is often classified as follows:

        1.   Cost--something that requires the use of business resources. May be incurred to obtain assets or expenses, or to fulfill obligations.

        2.   Benefit--something that provides business resources and/or reduces resource consumption. May be an increase in assets or revenues or decreases in obligations.

        3.   Generally, if the financial benefits of a particular action outweigh the costs, the course of action would usually be recommended.

        4.   Costs and benefits are not always financial. For example, actions may have psychological or environmental costs and benefits.

    B.   Management accounting information differs from financial accounting information. See Exhibit 2.12.

        1.   The management accounting subsystem often communicates nonfinancial data in the form of quantitative information not stated in dollars and cents. Some examples are number of labor hours, number of units sold, or number of defective units.

        2.   In a management accounting subsystem, the level of detail depends on the nature of the decisions being made.

            a.   Generally there is a greater need for aggregated data when there is a wide span of responsibility.

            b.   Generally there is a greater need for detailed data at lower organizational levels.

        3.   The form and content of internal reports vary with the user, the decisions, and company policy.

        4.   Internal accounting reports are generated in response to the needs of the respective users. External financial statements are issued periodically.

Problem I

Indicate whether the following statements are either true (T) or false (F).

___T___ 1. The corporate annual report is the primary source of information provided by a company to its stockholders and creditors.
___F___ 2. All external users are provided with the same type of accounting information.
___T___ 3. An accounting event does not occur until an exchange between two entities reaches the performance stage.
___F___ 4. Accumulated depreciation will be shown on the income statement.
___T___ 5. A benefit is an increase in assets or revenues or decrease in obligations.
___T___ 6. Internal accounting reports tend to be generated more frequently than external accounting reports.
___T___ 7. After every accounting event, total assets must equal total equities.
___T___ 8. Revenues increase the firm's obligation to its owners.
___F___ 9. For internal management reporting purposes, the level of detail provided will increase as the span of responsibility increases.

Problem II

Indicate the correct answer by circling the appropriate letter.

1. Which of the following accounting subsystems is designed to communicate information to external users, primarily stockholders and creditors?
   a. financial
   b. management
   c. tax
   d. regulatory

2. An obligation to transfer resources to others in the future is classified as a/an _____.
   a. asset
   b. revenue
   c. expense
   d. equity

3. An asset created by a manufacturing firm that represents the right to use partially completed products is _____.
   a. cost of goods sold
   b. work-in-process inventory
   c. supplies
   d. finished goods inventory

4. Which of the following is not shown on the balance sheet?
   a. assets
   b. liabilities
   c. owners' equity
   d. revenue

5. Which of the following accounting subsystems is designed to provide information to internal users?
   a. financial
   b. management
   c. tax
   d. regulatory

6. Which of the following would be shown on the income statement?
   a. assets
   b. liabilities
   c. revenues
   d. dividends

7. The financial statement designed to show the revenues generated, expenses incurred, and resulting net income for a period of time is the _____.
   a. balance sheet
   b. income statement
   c. statement of changes in retained earnings
   d. statement of changes in owners' equity

8. Assets that represent legal rights that are expected to last many years and have no physical substance are called _____.
   a. revenues
   b. expenses
   c. property, plant and equipment
   d. intangibles

Problem III

The following is a list of important ideas and key concepts from the chapter. To test your knowledge of these terms, match the term with the definition by placing the number in the space provided.

_7_	Accounting event	_24_	Liability
_2_	Annual report	_10_	Management accounting subsystem
_15_	Asset	_9_	Net income
_18_	Balance sheet	_4_	Owners' equity
_12_	Benefit	_21_	Property, plant, and equipment
_14_	Contributed capital	_17_	Regulatory accounting subsystem
_6_	Cost	_1_	Relevant information
_19_	Economic events	_20_	Residual interest
_11_	Equity	_5_	Revenue
_23_	Expense	_16_	Revenue event
_22_	Expense event	_8_	Statement of cash flows
_3_	Financial accounting subsystem	_13_	Statement of owners' equity

1. Information that is capable of making a difference in the user's decision

2. The report provided to stockholders and other external users that contains general information about the company as well as the financial statements for the fiscal period

3. The accounting subsystem designed for communicating with external users, primarily stockholders and creditors

4. The obligation to transfer resources to owners in the future after the liabilities have been met

5. The amount earned by a company for providing goods and services to customers

6. Something that requires business resources

7. An economic event that is specific to the entity, measurable, and changes the entity's rights and/or obligations

8. The financial statement designed to show the cash inflows and outflows from operating, investing, and financing activities for a period of time

9. The difference between revenue and expense in a certain time period

10. The accounting subsystem designed for communicating with internal users

---

11. Obligations of the business to transfer resources of the company at some time in the future

12. Something that provides business resources or reduces resource consumption

13. The financial statement designed to show the changes that occurred in owners' equity for a period of time covered by the income statement

14. The capital contributed by the owners that gives the owners the right to receive the residual resources of the company

15. A right to use resources with expected future economic benefits for the entity

16. An increase in assets or a decrease in liabilities and an increase in owners' equity resulting from the operations of the entity

17. The accounting subsystem designed for communicating with regulatory agencies such as the SEC

18. The financial statement designed to show the assets, liabilities and owners' equity of the entity at a particular point in time

19. A decision that when acted on affects an entity's wealth

20. The interest remaining after all the company's obligations have been met

21. Assets that have physical substance and are expected to be used many years

22. A decrease in assets or an increase in liabilities and a decrease in owners' equity resulting from the operations of the business

23. The amount incurred in an attempt to generate revenue

24. An obligation to transfer a measurable amount of resources or services to suppliers of goods and services

Problem IV

Complete the following sentences by filling in the correct response.

1. Assets, liabilities and owners' equity are shown on the _____.

2. An _____ event occurs when you make a decision that affects your wealth.

3. The requirement that accounting events must be measurable in financial terms is an application of the _____ concept.

4. If cash is not exchanged in a transaction between entities, the event is recorded at its _____.

5. If a business chooses to use net income generated from operations rather than pay dividends, it is known as _____ and is shown on the balance sheet.

6. _____ stakeholders use accounting information primarily to make decisions about future business operations, whereas _____ decisions are made primarily about how the business operated in the past.

7. The purpose of the _____ is to report to external users the net income of the business for a particular time.

8. The difference between revenues and expenses for a certain period of time is called _____.

9. The management accounting subsystem generally classifies accounting information as either a _____ or a _____.

10. What are the three qualities that an economic event must satisfy to be considered an accounting event?

    a. _____
    b. _____
    c. _____

Problem V

Match the right or obligation to the appropriate accounting classification by placing the letter in the space provided.

Right or Obligation

_____1. An obligation to pay employees for work performed
_____2. Owner's right to receive any assets remaining after business liabilities are met
_____3. Right to receive money from a customer for services provided
_____4. Term used to denote the right to sell merchandise owned by a company to customers
_____5. An obligation to pay suppliers for goods or services provided
_____6. Term used to denote the right to use assets, such as paper, pens, etc., in operations.
_____7. Term used to denote the right to use long lived assets, such as buildings, in operations
_____8. An obligation to repay amounts previously borrowed from a bank

Accounting Classification

A. accounts receivable   E. salaries payable
B. inventory   F. accounts payable
C. supplies   G. notes payable
D. property plant and equipment H. contributed capital

Pause and reflect:

Individuals are sometimes described as being either risk averse or risk seekers. In analyzing an investment opportunity, how do you think an individual's risk preference would affect his/her relative emphasis between a return of capital and a return on capital?

_____
_____
_____
_____
_____
_____
_____
_____
_____
_____
_____
_____

Problem VII

1. The following accounting events occurred during the first period of operations of Lanex Inc., a service firm. Using the matrix provided, show the effects of each accounting event on the company's assets, liabilities and owners' equity. The first accounting event has been recorded.

a) The owners invested $60,000 in the business.
b) Lanex purchases $600 of supplies to be used in the business. Payment is to be made in 30 days.
c) A building is purchased for $35,000.
d) Customers pay $6,000 to Lanex for services provided during the period.
e) Employees are paid $1,500 for services provided to Lanex during the period.
f) Customers are billed $3,600 for services provided during the period (payment has not been received).
g) At the end of the period, Lanex recognizes 1/20 of the cost ($35,000 x 1/20 = $1,750) of the building as depreciation expense.
h) Lanex uses $450 of the supplies purchased earlier in the period.

	Assets	=	Liabilities	+	Owners' Equity Contributed
	Cash				Capital
Events:					
a)	+60,000				+60,000
b)					
c)					
d)					
e)					
f)					
g)					
h)					
Ending Balances		=		+	

2. Zectar, Inc. purchases records for resale to customers. Beginning of the period balances are provided in the matrix below. Show the effects of each accounting event on the company's assets, liabilities and owners' equity. The first accounting event has been recorded.

a) Zectar received a $2,000 payment from a customer on services billed and performed in the previous period.
b) Inventory costing $16,000 was sold to a customer for $35,000.
c) Zectar paid $2,500 rent on its warehouse.
d) Zectar borrowed $20,000 from a local bank.
e) A $3,000 payment was made to a creditor for inventory purchased in the previous period.
f) Merchandise for resale to customers was purchased for $10,000.
g) Employees were paid $1,000 in salaries for services performed during the period.
h) At the end of the period, Zectar recognized 1/10 of the cost ($45,000 x 1/10 = $4,500) of the equipment as depreciation expense.
i) $500 in dividends were paid to owners.

		Assets			=	Liabilities	+	Owners' Equity	
	Cash	Accounts Receivable	Inventory	Equipment	Accumulated Depreciation		Accounts Payable	Contributed Capital	Retained Earnings
Beg. Bal.	$17,000	$3,400	$25,000	$45,000	<$9,000>	=	$3,500	$70,000	$7,900
Events:									
a)									
b)									
c)									
d)									
e)									
f)									
g)									
h)									
i)									
Ending Balance						=		+	

Solutions for Chapter 2

Problem 1

1.	T	6.	T
2.	F	7.	T
3.	T	8.	T
4.	F	9.	F
5.	T		

Problem II

1.	a	5.	b
2.	d	6.	c
3.	b	7.	b
4.	d	8.	d

Problem III

7	Accounting event	24	Liability
2	Annual report	10	Management accounting subsystem
15	Asset	9	Net income
18	Balance sheet	4	Owners' equity
12	Benefit	21	Property, plant, and equipment
14	Contributed capital	17	Regulatory accounting subsystem
6	Cost	1	Relevant information
19	Economic events	20	Residual interest
11	Equity	5	Revenue
23	Expense	16	Revenue event
22	Expense event	8	Statement of cash flows
3	Financial accounting subsystem	13	Statement of owners' equity

Problem IV

1. balance sheet
2. economic
3. monetary
4. cash equivalent
5. retained earnings
6. internal, stockholders'
7. income statement
8. net income
9. cost, benefit
10. a. Be specific to an economic entity
    b. Be capable of being measured in financial terms
    c. Have two effects that create or change the rights and obligations of the entity

Problem V

1. E	5. F
2. H	6. C
3. A	7. D
4. B	8. G

Pause and Reflect

A return of capital is the recovery of the original investment whereas a return on capital is the profit generated by the investment. For example, assume an investor purchased stock for $1,000 and later sold that stock for $1,020. The investor would have a return of capital of $1,000 and a return on capital of $20.

Generally, the more risky the investment, the greater is the opportunity for a large return on capital. However, there is also a greater chance that the investor will not recover his/her original investment (i.e. a negative return of capital). Therefore, a risk averse investor will choose an investment with a lower return on capital as long as the return of capital is relatively assured. On the other hand, a risk seeker is willing to lose all or a large portion of his/her original investment for the opportunity to earn a large return on capital.

Problem VII

1.

	Assets				=	Liabilities	+	Owners' Equity	
	Cash	Accounts Receivable	Supplies	Building	Accumulated Depreciation	Accounts Payable		Contributed Capital	Retained Earnings
Events:									
a)	+60,000							+60,000	
b)			+600			+600			
c)	-35,000			+35,000					
d)	+ 6,000								+6,000
e)	- 1,500								-1,500
f)		+3,600							+3,600
g)					-1,750				-1.750
h)			-450						- 450
Ending Balances	$29,500	$3,600	$150	$35,000	<$1,750>	= $600	+	$60,000	$5,900

Introduction to Accounting: An Integrated Approach, 1st Edition

2.

	Assets					=	Liabilities		+	Owners' Equity	
	Cash	Accounts Receivable	Inventory	Equipment	Accumulated Depreciation		Accounts Payable	Notes Payable		Contributed Capital	Retained Earnings
Beg. Bal.:	$17,000	$3,400	$25,000	$45,000	<$ 9,000>	=	$3,500		+	$70,000	$ 7,900
Events:											
a)	+ 2,000	-2,000									
b)	+35,000										+35,000
			-16,000								-16,000
c)	- 2,500										- 2,500
d)	+20,000							+20,000			
e)	- 3,000						-3,000				
f)	-10,000		+10,000								
g)	- 1,000										- 1,000
h)					- 4,500						- 4,500
i)	- 500										- 500
Ending Balance	$57,000	$1,400	$19,000	$45,000	<$13,500>	=	$ 500	$20,000	+	$70,000	$18,400

Chapter 3   Business Operations and Cycles

Learning Objective 1:

Identify the operating, investing, and financing activities of a business.

Summary

Operating activities are the profit-making activities of an organization. Investing activities include the purchase and sale of long-term assets and other major items used in a business's operations. Financing activities involve obtaining cash or other resources needed to pay for investments in long-term assets and to repay money borrowed from creditors and owners. Classifying activities depends on the nature of the business. See Exhibit 3.1.

Learning Objective 2:

Explain the purpose of internal controls in business.

Summary

A good system of internal controls has three characteristics: (1) promotes operational efficiency, (2) ensures the accuracy of the information in the accounting system, and (3) encourages management and employees to comply with applicable laws and regulations.

Learning Objective 3:

Describe the sequence of activities in the expenditure cycle.

Summary

The expenditure cycle includes four activities: (1) determining the business's needs for goods and services, (2) selecting vendors and ordering goods, (3) receiving, securing, and storing goods, and (4) paying for the goods and services received.

Learning Objective 4:

Explain the sequence of activities in the revenue cycle.

Summary

The revenue cycle includes five major activities: (1) generating customer orders, (2) approving customer credit for credit sales, (3) shipping goods to customers, (4) billing credit customers, and (5) collecting from customers.

Learning Objective 5:

Describe the sequence of activities in the conversion cycle.

Summary

The conversion cycle has four primary activities: (1) scheduling production, (2) requisitioning raw materials, (3) combining labor, machines, and other resources to make the goods, and (4) storing finished goods.

Learning Objective 6:

Identify the phases of the management cycle.

Summary

Businesses make and implement decisions in three phases: (1) planning phase, (2) performing phase, and (3) evaluating phase. In the planning phase, management determines its objectives and means of achieving those objectives. The performing phase consists of doing the planned activities, and in the evaluating phase management compares actual results with the plan.

Outline of Key Concepts

I. Business activities consist of operating, investing, and financing activities.

    A. Operating activities--the profit-making activities of the enterprise. They arise from revenue-generating and expense-increasing activities. Operating activities have two key aspects:

        1. They are more directly associated with profit making.

        2. They involve a series of transactions or events that occur regularly and routinely.

    B. Investing activities--include the purchase and sale of long-term assets in addition to other major items used in a business's operations.

    C. Financing activities--involve obtaining cash or other means needed to pay for investments in long-term assets and to repay money borrowed from creditors and owners.

    D. The relationship between the activities and the financial statements. See Exhibit 3.3.

        1. Operating activities are usually associated with the income statement, the cash flows statement, and the current assets section of the balance sheet.

        2. Investing and financing activities are identified most closely with items on the balance sheet and the cash flows statement.

II. A business must have a good system of internal control.

    A. Internal control system--set of policies and procedures designed to meet three objectives:

        1. Promote operational efficiency.

        2. Ensure the accuracy of information in the accounting system.

        3. Encourage management and employees to comply with applicable laws and regulations.

B. Important internal control procedures:

    1. Requiring proper authorization--persons responsible for certain activities have the authority to enforce the policies associated with the activities.

    2. Separating incompatible duties--dividing among employees the responsibility for duties that have the potential to allow for one person to violate company policies.

        a. Strive to separate the approval, execution, custody, and recording phases of a business transaction.

    3. Maintaining adequate documents and records--have documents and records that capture all the necessary information about a transaction in the most efficient and effective way possible.

    4. Physically controlling assets and documents--safeguarding both human and physical resources.

    5. Providing independent checks on performance--having another employee who was not involved in the original activity check the work.

III. A cycles' view of operating activities.

    A. Expenditure cycle--sequence of transactions, or activities, between a business and the suppliers from whom it acquires goods and services.

        1. There are two goals during the expenditure cycle:

            a. To receive the best quality goods and services, when needed, at the lowest possible price.

            b. To ensure timely payment for the goods and services.

        2. The expenditure cycle has four major activities:

            a. Determining the business's needs for goods and services.

            b. Selecting vendors and ordering goods.

                i. Assess service, quality, and price.

            c. Receiving, securing, and storing goods.

  d. Paying for goods and services received.

    i. Purchase discounts--reductions from the invoice price for payment by customers made within a period of time. They are incentives for the business to pay early.

B. Revenue cycle--a business and its customers are involved in a series of transactions where the customer receives goods or services and pays for them.

  1. The goals of the revenue cycle are:

    a. To sell the products the customer wants, in the quantities they want, at a competitive price.

    b. To receive payment from the customer within the invoice period.

  2. The revenue cycle consists of five activities:

    a. Generating customer orders--may be cash or credit.

    b. Approving customer credit--conduct a background check on how well the potential customer has paid debts in the past.

    c. Shipping goods to customers.

    d. Billing credit customers.

      i. Sales discount--allows the customer to pay less than the full amount of the invoice if the customer pays within a specified time period.

    e. Collecting from customers.

C. Conversion cycle--found only in manufacturing businesses. Requires the use of machines and other equipment along with employee labor to convert raw materials into products to be sold.

  1. Goal of the conversion cycle is to manufacture quality products that customers want at the time they want them at the lowest possible cost.

  2. The conversion cycle involves four primary activities:

    a. Scheduling production--scheduling the use of machines and arrival of materials is important in controlling and reducing costs.

b. Obtaining raw materials--materials and supplies are obtained through the expenditure cycle.

c. Making products--See Exhibit 3.12.

    i. Manufacturing overhead--cost of all manufacturing resources used to make products but not directly associated with production.

d. Storing finished goods--store goods for as short a time as possible to minimize storage costs and the investment in finished, unsold goods.

IV. Changes in the business environment have had an impact on manufacturing.

A. Development of global markets.

    1. Communication and transportation between nations faster and cheaper.

    2. Formation of free trade blocks, such as the North American Free Trade Agreement (NAFTA) and the European Union (EU).
        FR. GB. Belg. , Ir
    3. Availability of labor in low-wage countries vs. automation.

B. Customer-focused operations. Includes concepts like "user-friendly", zero defects, money-back guarantees.

C. Advances in manufacturing and communications technology. Includes computer-assisted design (CAD) of products, computer-assisted manufacturing (CAM), and computer-integrated manufacturing (CIM).

V. The management cycle involves making and implementing decisions. There are three phases.

    A.   Planning phase--management determines its objectives and the means of achieving those objectives.

        1.   Strategic plans--set the broad course for the business and cover relatively long periods of time.

        2.   Operating plans--plans for business activities usually for only one year at a time.

    B.   Performing phase--management implements the plan by doing the planned activities.

    C.   Evaluation phase--management compares the actual results achieved with the company's objectives.

Problem I

Indicate whether the following statements are either true (T) or false (F).

_____1.   Operating activities provide cash for both financing and investing activities of a business.

_____2.   A good system of internal controls prevents an employee from performing more than one phase of a business transaction.

_____3.   The expenditure cycle only occurs in manufacturing type firms.

_____4.   The conversion cycle is a sequence of events conducted within a business rather than between a company and an external party.

_____5.   The request for payment for goods or services delivered to the business is called a vendor's invoice.

_____6.   The acceptance of a purchase order by a vendor results in the creation of a legally binding contract.

_____7.   Credit sales are made when goods are delivered to the customer before the customer pays for them.

_____8.   The remittance advice serves as the contract between a freight carrier and the selling company.

_____9.   When products are shipped FOB destination, title of the goods passes when the goods are picked up by the common carrier.

_____10. When products are shipped FOB shipping point, the seller must pay any shipping charges.

_____11. The overriding factor in scheduling production is demand for the company's product.

_____12. U. S. based companies do not need to consider cultural differences when designing and marketing products.

_____13. Quality of products is the overriding goal in a customer-focused operation.

_____14. With advances in technology, labor has become a decreasing part of the cost of producing a product.

_____15. The development phase begins with initial product design and continues through the initial manufacture to delivery of the product to the first customer.

Problem II

Indicate the correct answer by circling the appropriate letter.

1. The sale of goods to a customer occurs in the _____ cycle.
    a. expenditure
    b. revenue
    c. conversion
    d. none of the above

2. Which of the following is not a primary activity associated with the expenditure cycle?
    a. determining the business needs for goods and services
    b. generating customer orders
    c. selecting a vendor and placing the order
    d. receiving, securing, and storing the goods

3. The document that provides the vendor with a list of what required items are needed and their quantities, in addition to other terms, like shipping dates is the _____.
    a. purchase requisition
    b. purchase order
    c. receiving report
    d. vendor's invoice

4. The purchase of inventory that will be sold to customers occurs in the _____ cycle.
    a. expenditure
    b. revenue
    c. conversion
    d. none of the above

Use the following information for the next three problems:

The Sunmark Company purchased $100,000 in inventory on account. The terms of the sale were 1/10,n/60.

5. If Sunmark pays the invoice within 10 days, the goods will cost _____.
    a. $40,000
    b. $99,000
    c. $100,000
    d. $101,000

6. If Sunmark pays the invoice at the end of 60 days, the goods will cost _____.
    a. $40,000
    b. $99,000
    c. $100,000
    d. $101,000

7. If Sunmark pays the invoice at the end of 60 days, the annualized interest cost of not taking the discount will be _____.
    a. 10%
    b. 37.2%
    c. 16.6%
    d. 7.4%

8. Adding a memory chip to a laptop computer will occur in the _____ cycle of a computer manufacturing company.
   a. expenditure
   b. revenue
   c. conversion
   d. none of the above

9. Which of the following is not considered a primary activity in the revenue cycle?
   a. generating customer orders
   b. approving customer credit for credit sales
   c. selecting a vendor and paying the order
   d. collecting from customers

10. The document which requests payment from the customer for goods or services supplied by the business is the _____.
    a. sales order
    b. purchase order
    c. sales invoice
    d. bill of lading

11. Onyx received a sales purchase order from LTD on December 1, 1996. The product was shipped December 27, 1996, terms FOB destination. The product arrived at LTD on January 3, 1997. Onyx received payment for the goods on January 31, 1997. In determining accounting net income, the sale will be reported on _____.
    a. December 1, 1996
    b. December 27, 1996
    c. January 3, 1997
    d. January 31, 1997

12. All of the following are primary activities of the conversion cycle except _____.
    a. scheduling production
    b. obtaining raw materials
    c. combining labor, machines, and other resources to make the goods
    d. collecting cash from customers

13. Which of the following costs would be considered manufacturing overhead?
    a. rent on machines used to cut metal plates for lawnmower engines
    b. utilities on the factory building
    c. engineering cost incurred to redesign the product
    d. all of the above are manufacturing overhead costs

14. A document that identifies the job or batch of products as it goes through the conversion process is the _____.
    a. bill of materials
    b. production order
    c. purchase order
    d. time ticket

15. The phase in which a company seeks new markets for its product is considered the

_____.
    a. start-up phase
    b. development phase
    c. decline phase
    d. evaluating phase

Problem III

The following is a list of important ideas and key concepts from the chapter. To test your knowledge of these terms, match the term with the definition by placing the number in the space provided.

_____	Business activities	_____	Operating plans
_____	Conversion cycle	_____	Paper trail
_____	Evaluating phase	_____	Performing phase
_____	Expenditure cycle	_____	Planning phase
_____	Free on board destination	_____	Product life cycle
_____	Internal control system	_____	Revenue cycle
_____	Machine setups	_____	Sales invoice
_____	Manufacturing overhead	_____	Segregation of incompatible duties
_____	Operating activities		

1. A bill sent by sellers to customers which includes the quantity and type of goods sold as well as the customer's purchase order

2. The course of product-related events, which begins with the idea for a new product and ends when the product is no longer sold

3. The profit-making activities of the enterprise

4. Plans for business activities to accomplish objectives during the next year

5. The series of business events in which the business exchanges assets for goods and services provided from suppliers

6. Shipping terms where the legal title to goods does not pass to the customer until he or she receives the goods

7. The first phase of the management cycle, where management determines its objectives and the means of achieving them

8. Dividing among employees, the responsibility for duties that make it easy for one person to violate company policies

9. The series of transactions in which businesses sell goods and services to customers and receive payment from customers

10. Events that involve making and carrying out investing, financing, and operating decisions that deal with business assets or obligations

11. The final phase of the management cycle comparing company operating activity results with planning activities which involves other standards to assess performance; input to future plans

12. The set of policies and procedures designed to promote operational efficiency, ensure the accuracy of accounting information, and encourage compliance with laws and regulations

13. The sequence of manufacturing events that combines raw materials with labor and other business assets to produce products

14. Adjustments made to machines to get them ready for production

15. The cost of all manufacturing resources used to make products that are not directly associated with production

16. The series of documents created to record information regarding various business transactions

17. The second phase of the management cycle, where the business actually performs its planned activities

Problem IV

1. What are the two factors that distinguish operating activities from investing and financing activities.

_____

_____

_____

_____

_____

_____

2. Describe three important ways that operating profits are used by a business.

_____

_____

_____

_____

_____

_____

3. What are the five procedures used in an internal accounting control system?

_____

_____

_____

_____

_____

_____

4. How does the goal of zero defects affect the production process in a manufacturing company?

_____

_____

_____

_____

_____

_____

_____

_____

_____

_____

_____

_____

_____

_____

Problem V

In the space provided, indicate whether the business activity is considered an operating activity (O), investing activity (I), or a financing activity (F).

_____1. The company purchased land to be used as a parking lot.
_____2. Inventory was sold to a customer for cash.
_____3. Legal services fees were performed for a customer. Payment is due in 30 days.
_____4. The company borrowed $20,000 from a local bank.
_____5. Raw materials are used in the production process to make paint.
_____6. A machine will be used by a construction company to install water lines is purchased for cash.
_____7. The company placed an advertisement in the newspaper.
_____8. A three-year flood insurance policy covering the factory building is purchased for cash.
_____9. Inventory for sale to customers is purchased on account. Payment is due in 30 days.
_____10. A warehouse that was no longer needed in the business was sold for cash.

Problem VI

The following activities occurred in Xectar Company, a small commercial and residential construction firm. In the space provided, indicate whether the activity occurred in the planning (PL), performing (PR) or the evaluating (E) phase of the management cycle.

_____1. Raw materials are purchased from a lumberyard.
_____2. The company decides to obtain a 10 percent market share for residential construction by the end of its third year of operations.
_____3. Advertisement is placed on a local radio station.
_____4. Due to high residential construction demands, the commercial division is closed and employees are transferred to the residential division.
_____5. Cash is collected from a customer.

Pause and reflect:

The book states that, for most businesses, the best policy is to always pay within the discount period even if it has to borrow the money. If a purchase discount is such a good deal for the purchaser, why is it offered by the seller?

_____
_____
_____
_____
_____
_____
_____
_____
_____
_____
_____
_____
_____
_____
_____
_____
_____
_____

Solutions for Chapter 3

Problem 1

1. T	9. F
2. T	10. F
3. F	11. T
4. T	12. F
5. T	13. T
6. T	14. T
7. T	15. F
8. F	

Problem II

1. b	9. c
2. b	10. c
3. b	11. c
4. a	12. d
5. b	13. d
6. c	14. b
7. d	15. b
8. c	

Problem III

10	Business activities	4	Operating plans
13	Conversion cycle	16	Paper trail
11	Evaluating phase	17	Performing phase
5	Expenditure cycle	7	Planning phase
6	Free on board destination	2	Product life cycle
12	Internal control system	9	Revenue cycle
14	Machine setups	1	Sales invoice
15	Manufacturing overhead	8	Segregation of incompatible duties
3	Operating activities		

Problem IV

1. Operating activities are more directly associated with profit making and they involve a series of transactions or events that occur regularly and frequently.

2. Operating profits are used (a) to pay for capital provided by owners and lenders, (b) to acquire goods and services for resale to customers, and (c) to acquire additional long-term assets.

3. The five procedures used in an internal accounting control system are (a) requiring proper authorization for transactions, (b) separating incompatible duties, (c) maintaining adequate documents and records, (d) physically controlling assets and documents, and (e) providing independent checks on performance.

4. The goal of zero defects has several implications for the manufacturing process. Often times products will be designed with fewer parts so that assembly is more simple and there are fewer opportunities for production mistakes. Employees are given the power to stop the production process when defects are detected. Thus, problems are corrected before more defective items are produced. Venders provide input into the production process to insure they understand how their products are being used and so they can make suggestions that will lead to cost savings.

Problem V

1. I
2. O
3. O
4. F
5. O
6. I
7. O
8. O
9. O
10. I

Problem VI

1. PR
2. PL
3. PR
4. E
5. PR

Pause and Reflect

When analyzed in annual percentage rate terms, the cost of offering discounts can be very high. If the seller is experiencing cash flow problems, it would appear that the company would be better off borrowing the money and not offering the discount. However, in deciding whether or not to offer discounts, the seller is dealing with a problem not faced by the purchaser. In addition to the issue of timing of cash flows, the seller must deal with customers who may not pay at all. If a customer is unable to pay all of its suppliers, it will probably pay the invoices that offer discounts before it pays those not offering discounts. So, from the seller's perspective, offering discounts may reduce its bad debts. The business problem then becomes, whether the reduction in bad debts (cash inflow) exceeds the discounts taken by customers (cash outflow). If the answer is yes, the company will be more profitable if it offers the sales discounts.

Chapter 4   Pricing, Costs, and Profit Planning

Learning Objective 1:

Explain the four primary influences on selling price and how a company determines its pricing strategy.

Summary

The four primary influences on selling price are customers, competition, legal constraints, and costs. Pricing is usually determined by one of two strategies: (1) market-based or (2) cost-based.

Learning Objective 2:

Describe the three cost behavior patterns and use the formula for a straight line to define each.

Summary

A fixed cost does not change in total as the amount of the cost driver increases, but it decreases per unit of cost driver as the amount of the cost driver increases. A variable cost changes in total in direct proportion to the change in the level of the cost driver. Variable costs remain constant on a per unit basis. Mixed costs have both variable and fixed components.

Learning Objective 3:

Understand how to predict costs using the high/low method.

Summary

The high/low method requires the use of the highest and lowest levels of the cost driver and the related costs at these levels. Divide the change in cost by the change in the amount of the cost driver to obtain the variable cost per unit of cost driver. Use the variable cost in the straight-line equation formula to determine the fixed cost.

Learning Objective 4:

Predict costs using linear regression analysis.

Summary

Regression analysis uses multiple data points and statistical analysis to determine the total cost line. The cost driver is identified as the independent variable, and the cost is identified as the dependent variable.

Learning Objective 5:

Use cost-volume-profit analysis to determine the relationships among selling price, cost, volume, and profit for a single-product firm.

Summary

Cost-volume-profit (CVP) analysis is the study of how costs and profits change in response to changes in the volume of goods or services provided to customers. CVP assumes that cost behavior patterns are related to the volume of units produced and sold, and it also assumes that revenue and cost can be expressed in linear relationships.

Learning Objective 6: (Appendix)

Use multiproduct cost-volume-profit analysis to determine the relationships among selling price, cost, volume, and profit for a multiproduct firm.

Summary

Multiproduct CVP analysis is based on the same assumptions as single-product CVP with one addition--the relative sales mix of the products produced and sold must remain constant. The analysis uses a weighted-average contribution margin.

Outline of Key Concepts

I. Determining selling price.

    A.   There are four primary influences on selling prices.

        1.   The quantity of goods or services demanded by customers is influenced by selling price. In addition, service and quality affect the quantity demanded.

        2.   The quantity of product supplied and the selling prices charged by competitors affect selling price. Seller may operate in an environment of pure competition or monopolistic competition.

        3.   Legal, political, and social factors influence selling prices. Legal constraints are imposed on monopolies and oligopolies.

        4.   Costs to produce and distribute a product impact selling prices. The selling price must be high enough to cover costs and provide a profit to the owners.

    B.   Companies usually determine prices based on one of two strategies:

        1.   Prices are based on the market, subject to the constraint that the price cover long-run costs.

        2.   Prices are based on costs, subject to the constraints of customers, competitors, and legal/social factors.

        3.   There are a number of schemes for implementing these strategies. Examples are price skimming, penetration pricing, life-cycle pricing, and target pricing.

II. Understanding cost behavior.

    A.   Cost behavior patterns are defined in terms of a straight-line relationship within a specific range of operating activity known as the relevant range.

        1.   The formula for a straight line is $Y = m(X) + b$, where m represents the slope and b represents the intercept on the Y-axis.

        2.   For cost behavior analysis, Y = cost, m = variable cost per unit, and b = fixed cost.

B.   Cost drivers are activity measures that reflect the consumption of resources.   The consumption of resources causes cost to change.

C.   Fixed costs do not change in total as the amount of cost driver changes. Fixed costs decrease per unit of cost driver as the cost driver increases. The fixed cost formula is

$$Y = (0)X + b.$$

D.   Variable costs change in total in direct proportion to the changes in the level of cost driver. When measured on a per unit basis, variable costs are constant. The variable cost formula is

$$Y = (m)X + 0.$$

E.   Mixed costs vary in total in the same direction as the change in cost driver, but not in direct proportion to the change in the level of cost driver. Mixed costs increase in total but decrease per unit as the cost driver increases. The mixed cost formula is

$$Y = (m)X + b.$$

III.   Using cost estimation techniques to estimate future costs.

A.   The high/low method uses the highest and lowest levels of the cost and the related costs at those levels.

1.   The change in cost is divided by the change in the amount of the cost driver to determine the variable cost per unit of cost driver. The variable cost per unit is substituted into the straight-line formula to determine the fixed cost.

2.   The high-low method requires only two points which may be a problem if the data points are not representative of normal costs.

B.   Linear regression analysis is a method that uses multiple data points and statistical analysis to determine the total cost line.

1.   The line obtained from linear regression analysis is the most accurate representation of the linear relationship between the cost driver and the related costs.

2.   When using linear regression to estimate costs, the cost driver is referred to as X or the independent variable.   Total cost is referred to as Y or the dependent variable.

3. The linear regression output includes the estimated fixed cost for the period, the estimated variable cost per cost driver (X coefficient), and various statistical measures of how good the regression equation fits the cost data.

   a. R-squared measures the strength of the relationship between the cost driver and the cost. It ranges from 0 to 1, with 1 indicating a perfect predictor.

   b. Other measures include the standard error of the X coefficient and the *t* statistic.

IV. Cost-volume-profit (CVP) analysis is the study of how costs and profits change in response to changes in the volume of goods or services provided to customers. CVP assumes that cost behavior patterns are related to the volume of units produced and sold.

A. The assumptions of CVP analysis are:

   1. Selling price remains constant per unit regardless of the volume sold.

   2. Variable cost remains constant per unit regardless of the volume produced and sold.

   3. Fixed cost remains constant in total throughout the relevant range regardless of the volume produced and sold.

   4. For manufacturing firms, the number of units produced equals the number of units sold; for merchandising firms, the number of units purchased equals the number of units sold during the period.

   5. If more than one product is sold, the sales mix remains constant.

B. Defining revenue, cost, and profit in CVP.

   1. Total revenue = Selling price per unit x Number of units sold.

   2. Total cost = Variable cost per unit x Number of units sold + Fixed costs.

   3. Profit = Total revenue - Total costs.

   4. Total contribution margin = Total revenue - Total variable costs.

C. Performing CVP analysis (single product).

   1. Breakeven point--total revenue equals total cost.

        a.   The point at which the company does not make any profit nor suffer any loss.

        b.   Where total contribution margin equals total fixed costs.

        c.   See Exhibit 4.14 for a graphical approach to breakeven analysis.

   2.   May use a mathematical approach to CVP analysis.

        a.   Total revenue - Total variable costs - Total fixed cost = 0.

        b.   Contribution margin ratio--contribution margin per unit divided by the selling price per unit or the total contribution margin divided by the total revenue.

        c.   May determine a target profit level by substituting the desired profit for 0 in the breakeven equation. Total revenue - Total variable costs - Total fixed cost = Targeted profit level.

        d.   Before-tax profit = Desired profit after taxes/1- tax rate.

   3.   Sensitivity analysis is the process of changing the key variable in CVP analysis to determine how the CVP relationships react to changes in these variables.

        a.   May use sensitivity analysis to study the effect of changes in selling price, changes in variable cost, changes in fixed cost and changes in tax rates.

V. Appendix--Multiple-Product Cost-Volume-Profit Analysis.

   A.   Is guided by the same assumptions as single-product CVP, but there is one additional assumption: the relative sales mix must remain constant within the relevant range.

   B.   Performing multi-product CVP analysis.

     1.   Weighted-average contribution margin--calculated by multiplying the contribution margins of each individual product by the relative sales mix of that product and then add them all together.

     2.   Breakeven point in product mix--divide the weighted-average contribution margin into the fixed costs.

     3.   The quantity of an individual product sold at breakeven--multiply the breakeven point in product mix by the relative sales mix for each individual product.

Problem I

Indicate whether the following statements are either true (T) or false (F).

_____ 1. As the price for a product is increased, the demand for that product will also increase.
_____ 2. The higher the R-squared, the stronger is the relationship between the cost driver and the cost.
_____ 3. In a purely competitive market, a company will be a price taker.
_____ 4. A life-cycle pricing strategy may result in losses in the early stages of the product's life.
_____ 5. A mixed cost will increase in total but decreases per unit as the cost driver increases.
_____ 6. A weakness of the linear regression method of estimating costs is that it only uses two data points in its analysis.
_____ 7. In linear regression, the cost driver will be considered the independent variable.
_____ 8. Cost-volume-profit analysis assumes a linear relationship between cost and the number of units produced.
_____ 9. As fixed costs decrease, the breakeven point in sales dollars will increase.
_____ 10. An increase in the effective tax rate will cause a company's breakeven point in sales dollars to increase.

Problem II

Indicate the correct answer by circling the appropriate letter.

1. An environment in which a few firms control the types or distribution of products and services is a/an _____.
   a. monopoly
   b. oligopoly
   c. cartel
   d. none of the above

2. Which of the following is not a primary influence on a company's selling price?
   a. competition
   b. legal constraints
   c. product costs
   d. all of the above are primary influences

3. Glutton Motor Company uses a cost-based pricing policy in determining the sales prices of its cars. Glutton requires of all of its salespersons a minimum markup of 20 percent. If a new Ford Explorer cost Glutton $23,000, what is the minimum sales price that will be approved by management?
   a. $23,000
   b. $23,500
   c. $25,460
   d. $27,600

4. Inflex Corporation has finished the design of a new high resolution computer monitor. To gain market share, Inflex intends to sell the monitor below its cost of production. After a 5 percent market share has been attained, it will raise its price. What price setting strategy is Inflex practicing?
   a. penetration pricing
   b. life-cycle pricing
   c. target pricing
   d. none of the above

Use the following cost date for the next two questions:

Xene Company has provided the following quarterly data for the past two years on its maintenance costs:

	Cost Driver Machine Hours	Total Costs Maintenance Costs
1	3,500	$4,800
2	2,800	$3,900
3	4,500	$5,800
4	2,900	$4,200
5	5,200	$6,000
6	3,400	$4,200
7	4,700	$5,700
8	3,900	$5,300

5. Using the high/low method, Xene's estimated fixed maintenance cost is _____ per quarter.
   a. $1,450
   b. $1,875
   c. $2,600
   d. $3,900

6. Xene estimates that 5,000 machine hours will be needed in the next quarter to meet customer demands for its product. Using the high/low method, what will be the total estimated maintenance cost for the quarter?

    a. $4,500
    b. $5,200
    c. $5,825
    d. $6,150

7. Which of the following is not an assumption of cost-volume-profit analysis?
    a. In the short-run, facilities can be expanded or abandoned.
    b. Selling price remains constant per unit regardless of the volume sold.
    c. Variable cost remains constant per unit regardless of the volume produced and sold.
    d. For manufacturing firms, the number of units produced equals the number of units sold.

Use the following information for the next four problems:

Ducks Limited sells hand crafted duck decoys for $40. A supplier has agreed to sell the decoys to Ducks Limited for $23 per decoy. The company rents all of its office equipment and its building for $3,000 per month. All salespersons work for a straight commission of $2 per decoy sold.

8. The contribution margin ratio is _____.

    a. 67.5%
    b. 37.5%
    c. 32.5%
    d. 17.75%

9. The breakeven point in terms of units sold per month is _____.
    a. 200 units
    b. 250 units
    c. 300 units
    d. 400 units

10. If the company's goal is to generate $15,000 in pre-tax profits per month, its total dollar sales must be _____.
    a. $25,000
    b. $35,000
    c. $48,000
    d. $64,000

11. Assume that the company is subject to a 30% tax rate and its goal is to generate $7,000 per month in after-tax profits. How many units must Ducks Limited sell?

    a. 612
    b. 867
    c. 925
    d. 1,100

12. Mirex sells a product for $50 per unit. The variable cost per unit is $20 and total fixed costs are $120,000 per year. Mirex's supplier has indicated that cost per unit will increase to $22 next year. As a result of the cost increase, Mirex's new breakeven point in terms of sales dollars will be _____?

    a. $200,000
    b. $214,286
    c. $217,680
    d. $222,567

Problem III

The following is a list of important ideas and key concepts from the chapter. To test your knowledge of these terms, match the term with the definition by placing the number in the space provided.

_____ Breakeven point	_____ Penetration pricing
_____ Cartel	_____ Price fixing
_____ Contribution margin	_____ Price skimming
_____ Cost driver	_____ Price taker
_____ Fixed cost	_____ Pure competition
_____ Life-cycle pricing	_____ Relevant range
_____ Markup	_____ Sales mix
_____ Mixed (semi-variable) cost	_____ Sensitivity analysis
_____ Monopolistic competition	_____ Target pricing
_____ Monopoly	_____ Variable cost

_____1.   The expected range of operating activity; the range of activity used in gathering data for high/low or linear regression analysis

_____2.   A pricing strategy in which a company sets its selling price low initially to gain a share of the market

_____3.   The means of measuring activity that reflects consumption of resources; that which causes costs to change

_____ 4. A cost that varies in total in proportion to the change in cost driver level but is fixed per unit of cost driver throughout the relevant range

_____ 5. A strategy in which the company determines whether and how to produce a product at a cost that provides a certain selling margin

_____ 6. A company that has exclusive control over products, services, or geographic markets

_____ 7. The point at which total revenues equal total costs, total contribution margin equals total fixed costs, and the point where a company makes no profit and incurs no loss

_____ 8. A monopolistic combination of businesses

_____ 9. The relative proportions of units of products sold in a multiple-product company

_____ 10. An environment where a large number of sellers produce and distribute virtually identical products and services

_____ 11. The difference between revenue and variable costs

_____ 12. The process of changing a key variable in the cost-volume-profit relationship to examine the effects of the change on the other variables

_____ 13. In pure competition, a company that must accept the price offered by the market

_____ 14. A cost that is constant in total as the amount of the cost driver changes

_____ 15. A pricing strategy in which the company determines the selling price for the life of the product; it can be set below initial product cost

_____ 16. The additional amount added to the cost of the product to compute the selling price

_____ 17. A pricing strategy in which the company initially sets high selling prices to attract customers who are willing to pay more to receive the product first

_____ 18. An environment in which there are a large number of sellers with similar products

_____ 19. A cost that varies in the same direction as a cost driver and has both a fixed and a variable component

_____ 20. A pricing method by which a group of companies agree to limit supply and charge identical prices for their goods and services

Problem IV

Complete the following sentences by filling in the correct response.

1. As the price for a company's product is decreased, the demand for the product will
_____.

2. In a purely competitive market, prices are a function of _____ and _____.

3. Legal constraints are more likely to be imposed on industries whose competitive environment is either a _____ or an _____.

4. A _____ cost changes in total in direct proportion to changes in the cost driver. However, when measured on a per unit basis, the costs are _____.

5. The _____ _____ is the span of activity that is considered normal for a business.

6. In the long run, a company must set a price that covers its _____ and provides a _____ to the owners.

7. All pricing strategies are dependent on a company's ability to predict future _____ as well as _____ forces.

8. A _____ cost does not change in total as the cost driver changes. However, the cost per unit _____ as the cost driver increases.

9. A mixed cost has both a _____ and a _____ cost component.

10. _____ _____ is a cost estimation method that uses multiple data points and statistical analysis to determine the total cost line.

11. Under cost-volume-profit analysis, a profit report prepared for internal users divides costs into _____ costs and _____ costs.

Problem V

1. The following data are available for shipping costs incurred by the Amex Company. The regression output was obtained from the data input into Lotus 1-2-3:

	Units Shipped	Total Shipping Costs		
January	12,000	$26,500	Regression Output:	
February	11,000	$23,500	Constant	4110.396
March	15,000	$34,900	X Coefficient(s)	1.805
April	10,000	$21,000	Std Err of Coefficient	0.238
May	7,000	$17,300	R Squared	0.852
June	8,500	$20,100		
July	9,000	$19,000		
August	13,000	$24,500		
September	12,500	$25,000		
October	11,800	$24,900		
November	8,800	$21,000		
December	8,300	$20,700		

a. Using the high/low method, indicate the cost formula that represents the data.

b. Using the regression output, indicate the cost formula that represents the data.

2. Yourhat Inc. has just started a business which makes custom hats for sports teams. Hats are purchased from suppliers for $4.50 per hat. Yourhat then makes a team logo which is sewn on the hat at a total cost of $1.50 per hat. Yourhat's only other costs are annual fixed costs estimated to be $30,000. Based on a marketing study, Yourhat expects to be able to sell its hats for $10 each.

a. How many hats will have to be sold for Yourhat to break even?

b. If Yourhat wishes to reach an annual pre-tax profit of $200,000, its total dollar sales must be how much?

c. Assume that Yourhat is subject to a 35% effective tax rate. How many hats must be sold to earn after-tax profits of $175,000?

d. Congress is currently considering adopting a flat tax of 20%. If such legislation was adopted, how many hats must be sold to earn the $175,000 in profits referred to in (c) above?

Pause and Reflect:

Because computer programs can easily perform regression analysis, why shouldn't a manager collect data for numerous possible cost drivers and run regressions until the "best" model emerges?

_____
_____
_____
_____
_____
_____
_____
_____
_____
_____
_____
_____
_____
_____

Solutions for Chapter 4

Problem 1

1.	F	6.	F
2.	T	7.	T
3.	T	8.	T
4.	T	9.	F
5.	T	10.	F

Problem II

1.	b	7.	a
2.	d	8.	b
3.	d	9.	a
4.	a	10.	c
5.	a	11.	b
6.	c	12.	b

Problem III

7	Breakeven point	2	Penetration pricing
8	Cartel	20	Price fixing
11	Contribution margin	17	Price skimming
3	Cost driver	13	Price taker
14	Fixed cost	10	Pure competition
15	Life-cycle pricing	1	Relevant range
16	Markup	9	Sales mix
19	Mixed (semi-variable) cost	12	Sensitivity analysis
18	Monopolistic competition	5	Target pricing
6	Monopoly	4	Variable cost

Part IV

1. increase
2. supply, demand
3. monopoly, oligopoly
4. variable, constant
5. relevant range
6. costs, profit
7. costs, market
8. fixed, decreases
9. fixed, variable
10. linear regression
11. fixed, variable

Problem V

1. a.

	Units Shipped	Total Shipping Costs
High	15,000	$34,900
Low	<7,000>	<$17,300>
Difference	8,000	$17,600

$$\frac{\$17,600}{8,000} = \$2.20 \text{ per unit shipped}$$

Total shipping costs = ($2.20 x units shipped) + fixed costs

$34,900 = ($2.20 x 15,000) + fixed costs

fixed costs = $1,900

Cost Formula:
Total shipping costs = ($2.20 x units shipped) + $1,900

b. Cost Formula:
Total shipping costs = ($1.805 x units shipped) + $4,110

2. a. $\dfrac{FC}{CMPU} = Q$ $\dfrac{\$30,000}{\$4.00} = 7,500 \text{ units}$

b. $\dfrac{FC + P}{CMR} = \$$ $\dfrac{\$30,000 + \$200,000}{.40} = \$575,000$

c. $\dfrac{FC + \dfrac{P}{(1-\text{Tax rate})}}{CMPU} = Q$ $\dfrac{\$30,000 + \dfrac{\$175,000}{(1 - .35)}}{\$4.00} = 74,808$

d. $\dfrac{FC + \dfrac{P}{(1-\text{Tax rate})}}{CMPU} = Q$ $\dfrac{\$30,000 + \dfrac{\$175,000}{(1 - .20)}}{\$4.00} = 62,188$

Pause and Reflect

Collecting and preparing data for use in regression analysis is not without cost. Collecting data from numerous sources could cost more than the benefits obtained from finding a "best" model to estimate costs. In addition, management expects that a cause/effect relationship exists between the cost driver and cost. If numerous drivers are tried, it is possible that an accidental or spurious relationship may be selected as the model.

Chapter 5 Planning and Budgeting for Operating Activities

Learning Objective 1:

Explain why companies use budgets.

Summary

A budget is a plan for the future expressed in financial terms. Companies budget because they receive benefits in the areas of planning, communication and coordination, resource allocation, and control and evaluation.

Learning Objective 2:

Describe the various budgeting strategies companies use.

Summary

Mandated budgeting is a top-down budgeting strategy. Budget standards are established by upper-level managers. Participative budgeting, also known as bottom-up budgeting allows individuals affected by the budget to have input into the budgeting process. The budget numbers may be determined by either an incremental budgeting approach or a zero-based budgeting approach.

Learning Objective 3:

Explain the planning process in the revenue cycle and the resulting budgets.

Summary

The first step in the planning process in the revenue cycle is to estimate the volume of sales of goods or services at an expected selling price. A sales budget is developed from the sales planning activities. After the sales budget is determined, cash receipts from customers must be estimated. A cash receipts schedule reflects anticipated cash collections from customers.

Learning Objective 4:

Describe the planning process in the conversion cycle and the resulting budgets.

Summary

Conversion cycle planning has four parts: (1) scheduling production, (2) obtaining raw materials, (3) scheduling labor, and (4) planning manufacturing. A significant issue in conversion cycle planning is determining the amount and timing of finished goods, work-in-process, and raw materials inventories. A production budget results from the conversion cycle planning process.

Learning Objective 5:

Explain the planning process in the expenditure cycle and the resulting budgets.

Summary

After completing the production budget, a company must plan its raw materials purchases, labor requirements, and other resource requirements. This planning results in a direct materials purchases budget and a direct labor and manufacturing overhead budget. Companies must also plan for other expenditures, such as selling and administrative costs. The expenditure cycle concludes with the payment for goods and services. A cash disbursements schedule reflects these planned expenditures.

Learning Objective 6:

Describe the relationships of the revenue, conversion, and expenditure cycle budgets to the cash budget and pro forma financial statements.

Summary

The budgets prepared during the revenue, conversion, and expenditure cycle planning provide information for the preparation of the cash budget and pro forma financial statements.

Learning Objective 7: (Appendix)

Indicate the purpose of the economic order quantity model of inventory planning.

Summary

The economic order quantity (EOQ) model is a mathematical model that minimizes the total of short-term ordering costs plus short-term carrying costs for the period. It indicates the size of the order to place every time inventory is ordered.

Outline of Key Concepts

I. Budgeting is a process of expressing company goals and objectives in quantitative terms.

    A.   Budgeting offers a number of benefits.

        1.   Budgeting enhances the planning process by requiring planners to consider possible future courses of action and the resources needed to accomplish the activities.

        2.   Budgeting promotes communication and coordination among divisions or departments of a company.

        3.   Because organizations operate with limited resources, budgeting assists in resource allocation. A budget is useful in identifying value-added versus nonvalue-added activities.

        4.   A budget serves as a benchmark against which to evaluate and control performance.

    B.   Costs are associated with budgeting.

        1.   Budgeting consumes time and human energy.

        2.   Rigid adherence to the budget inhibits a business segment from responding to changes in the business environment.

        3.   Budgets and the budget process affect the motivation and behavior of individuals. This may result in budgetary slack, padding the budget, or employee resistance.

II. Budgetary strategy is how a company approaches the budgeting process.

    A.   Mandated budgeting--top management develops the budgets and passes them down the organizational hierarchy.

        1.   Little or no input is received from lower levels of management and employees.

        2.   Budget may be based on ideal standards or normal standards.

    B.   Participative budgeting--individuals affected by the budget have input into the budgeting process. Upper-level management coordinates the information received from lower levels and develops a comprehensive budget plan.

C. Incremental budgeting--use the current period's budget as a starting point in preparing the next period's budget.

D. Zero-based budgeting--begin each budget period with a zero budget. It requires study of each activity undertaken by the segment to see if it is necessary.

III. Operational planning in the revenue cycle is the first phase of the master budgeting process.. See Exhibit 5.1.

A. Sales planning is the first step in revenue cycle planning. Tools in sales planning include:
  1. Analysis of past sales levels and trends.

  2. Surveys of current and potential customers' needs.

  3. Demographic analysis of customers.

  4. Analysis of economic, political, legal, and social trends.

  5. Analysis of competitive trends.

  6. Analysis of planned advertising and promotion.

  7. After consideration of these issues, the sales budget is developed.

B. The second step in revenue cycle planning is to estimate cash receipts. To estimate cash receipts, the company must consider two issues:

  1. The amount that will be collected from customers.

  2. The timing of cash collections.

  3. The cash receipts schedule reflects the outcomes of these considerations.

IV. For a manufacturer, conversion cycle (production) planning follows revenue cycle planning. Conversion cycle planning consists of four components: scheduling production, obtaining raw materials, scheduling labor, and planning manufacturing overhead.

A. Planning inventory levels is an important element of conversion cycle planning. Involves balancing the short-run inventory ordering costs and the short-run costs of carrying one additional unit in the inventory for the period.

B. Just-in-time (JIT) inventory model--a long-run model based on the concept that inventory should arrive just as needed for production in the quantities needed.

    1. In the long run, carrying costs will exceed ordering costs, so it is best to maintain zero or minimal inventories.

    2. Pull system--production is determined (pulled by) customer demand, and the need for raw materials is determined (pulled by) production.

    3. Implications of JIT include:

        a. Sales estimates must be accurate.

        b. Production must be completed with zero or minimal defects.

        c. Company must have a strong relationship with its suppliers.

        d. Company must have a good relationship with its employees.

        e. Company must have a good relationship with its customers.

C. Conversion cycle planning culminates in the production budget.

V. Expenditure cycle planning is the third phase of the master budgeting process.

A. Manufacturers must plan expenditures for the resources required for production.

    1. Based upon the production budget, a company must plan its needs for direct materials and indirect materials. Combining the need for direct materials with desired inventory levels provides the information for the direct materials purchases budget.

    2. The production budget also serves as the basis for planning direct labor, indirect labor, and other resource needs. The output of this planning process is the direct labor and manufacturing overhead budget.

B. All companies plan for selling and administrative costs, such as salespersons' commissions, advertising, and rent.

    1. The department that supplies the resources typically does the planning.

    2. Planning results in a selling and administrative costs budget.

C. Expenditure cycle concludes with the payment for goods and services. Use information from the other expenditure cycle budgets as the basis for the cash disbursement schedule.

VI. The cash budget and pro forma financial statements are the culmination of revenue, conversion, and expenditure cycle planning.

A. Cash budget--shows the amounts of cash expected to be provided and used by operating activities during the coming year.

1. Information is drawn from the cash receipts and cash disbursements schedules.

2. The budget will also reflect the planned cash inflows and outflows from financing and investing activities.

B. Pro forma financial reports show the results of expected operations as outlined in the master budget process.

1. Pro forma profit report shows the expected revenues and expenses from the various budgets.

2. Pro forma balance sheet shows actual balances of a company's assets, liabilities, and owners' equity at the beginning of the budget period and the expected balances at the end of the budget period.

VII. Appendix--Economic Order Quantity Model (EOQ).

    A.   EOQ--a mathematical model that minimizes the total of short-term ordering costs plus short-term carrying costs for the period. It indicates the size of the order to place every time inventory is ordered. The assumptions include:

        1.   Demand is uniform throughout the year.

        2.   Lead time is constant throughout the year.

        3.   The entire order is received at one time; no partial orders.

        4.   No quantity discounts are offered by suppliers.

        5.   Inventory size is not limited.

        6.   Fixed storage costs are irrelevant.

    B.   Reorder point--inventory level that indicates the need to place an order for additional inventory. Based on estimates of daily demand of inventory, lead time for an order, and safety stock of inventory.

Problem I

Indicate whether the following statements are either true (T) or false (F).

_____1. The primary purpose of a budget is to present and describe the financial ramifications of plans for the future.

_____2. Raw materials used to produce a product would be considered a nonvalue-added activity.

_____3. The budgeting process promotes communication and coordination among divisions or departments within a company.

_____4. The cost of human capital is relatively small in the budget process.

_____5. Mandated budgets are most appropriate for product lines in the maturity or declining phases of the product life-cycle.

_____6. Incremental budgeting tends to be less time consuming than zero-based budgeting.

_____7. A strategic budget covers a longer time period than an operational budget.

_____8. Storing inventory is a nonvalue-added activity.

_____9. In large organizations, sales planning is usually done by the accounting department.

_____10. Under a JIT inventory system, little or no inventory is maintained.

Problem II

Indicate the correct answer by circling the appropriate letter.

1. Which of the following is not a primary benefit of budgeting?
    a. more effective planning
    b. improved communication and coordination between departments
    c. enhanced resource allocation
    d. all of the above are primary benefits of budgeting

2. All-Tire manufacturing company projects sales of 10,000, 14,000, and 18,000 tires, respectively, in its first three months of operations. All-Tire's bills customers on the first of the following month and credit terms are 3/10,n/30 from the invoice date. Forty percent of its customers are expected to pay within the discount period. An additional 50 percent will pay within 30 days (but after the discount period) and the remaining 10 percent will pay within 60 days. If tires sell for $50 each, what is All-Tire's expected cash receipts for the third month?
    a. $1,028,600
    b. $900,000
    c. $671,600
    d. $593,560

3. Which of the following is not a component of conversion cycle planning?
   a. scheduling production
   b. obtaining raw materials
   c. scheduling labor
   d. determining collection patterns of cash receipts

Use the following information for the next two questions:

Alnon Inc. manufactures and sells aluminum gates. Each gate requires 10 pounds of high-grade cast aluminum. The quarterly production budget for the first year of operations is as follows:

	1st Qtr	2nd Qtr	3rd Qtr	4th Qtr
Gates to be produced	11,000	15,000	12,000	9,000

4. Alnon has no raw materials on hand at the beginning of the first quarter. Alnon's policy is to maintain an ending inventory equal to 10% of the next quarter's estimated production. How many pounds of aluminum must Alnon purchase in the second quarter?
   a. 147,000 lbs.
   b. 150,000 lbs.
   c. 167,000 lbs.
   d. 135,000 lbs.

5. High-grade aluminum costs $1 per pound. Alnon pays for 50% of its purchases within the discount period (2/10,n/30) and another 30% are paid within the same quarter but after the discount period. The remaining 20% of the quarterly purchases are paid in the next quarter. Budgeted cash disbursements for the first quarter are _____.
   a. $98,750
   b. $100,000
   c. $110,000
   d. $122,500

Problem III

Following is a list of important ideas and key concepts from the chapter. To test your knowledge of these terms, match the term with the definition by placing the number in the space provided.

_____ Budgeting	_____ Normal standard
_____ Budgetary slack	_____ Padding the budget
_____ Direct labor	_____ Participative budgeting
_____ Direct materials	_____ Pro forma financial reports
_____ Ideal standard	_____ Project budgeting
_____ Incremental budgeting	_____ Pull system
_____ Indirect labor	_____ Stockout cost
_____ Indirect materials	_____ Strategic budget
_____ Master budgeting	_____ Zero-based budgeting

1. The process of compiling budgets prepared during revenue, conversion, and expenditure cycle planning that culminates in the cash budget and pro forma financial statements.

2. The difference between a chosen estimate of revenues or expenses and a realistic estimate

3. A production system in which goods are manufactured as needed by customers; demand "pulls" the system

4. The process of determining the specific resources provided by, and needed for, a specific project for the budgeting period

5. A budgeting strategy in which the company begins each budget period at zero and must justify all its activities proposed for the budget

6. A forecast prepared for a 5- to 10-year period that reflects the long-term planning of the company and is more general in nature than the operational budget.

7. The cost of materials used in production that cannot be traced directly to the finished products or whose cost does not warrant tracing

8. The process of expressing the company's goals and objectives in quantitative terms

9. The cost of the employees who manufacture the products

10. The company's cost of running out of inventory, which includes lost sales, customer ill will, and production slowdowns

11. The financial reports prepared for internal use that show the expected results of operations

12. The practice of overestimating time or cost required to complete an activity

13. The cost of the materials that can be traced directly to the finished products and whose cost warrants tracing them

14. A standard based on perfection or near ideal operating conditions

15. A budgeting system that allows individuals who are affected by the budget to have input into the budgeting process; budgets are developed at lower levels of management and employees and passed up to upper levels of management

16. A budgeting strategy in which a company begins the next budgeting period by using the current period's budget numbers as a benchmark

17. A standard based on normal, practical operating conditions

18. The cost of production employees whose efforts are necessary to manufacture products but who do not actually produce the products.

Problem IV

Complete the following sentences by filling in the correct response.

1. The _____ _____ determines what material is to be collected and is responsible for preparation of the budget.

2. _____ budgeting is most appropriate for divisions with product lines in the developmental or growth stage.

3. A budget serves as a useful benchmark against which to _____ and _____ actual performance.

4. In allocating resources within a company, _____ activities should be reduced or eliminated.

5. _____ budgeting is a top-down approach in which upper-level management sets budget levels.

6. The _____ _____ is the current plan for achieving the long-term goals and objectives of the company.

7. The first step in operational planning in the revenue cycle is to develop the _____ budget.

8. Indirect _____ and _____ are included in manufacturing overhead.

9. The _____ budget shows the amount of cash expected to be provided and used in operations and the cash inflows and outflows from financing and investing activities.

Part V

The following budgets have been prepared for Bill's merchandising firm for the first quarter of the year:

Sales Budget for the Period January -- March			
	January	February	March
Sales (units)	5,000	7,000	6,000
Sales (dollars)	$50,000	$70,000	$60,000

Purchases Budget for the Period January -- March

	January	February	March
Sales (dollars)	$50,000	$70,000	$60,000
Cost of sales	$25,000	$35,000	$30,000
Add desired ending inventory	$14,000	$12,000	$15,000
Cost of goods available	$39,000	$47,000	$45,000
Less beginning inventory		$14,000	$12,000
Purchases required	$39,000	$33,000	$33,000

Selling and administrative expenses are projected at $10,000 per month and are paid in the same month as incurred. Estimated collections of sales are 60% during the month of sale and 40% during the following month. Purchases are paid 80% during the month of purchase and 20% during the following month. There are no projected investing or financing cash inflows or outflows during the first quarter.

Required: Prepare the cash budget for the first three months of the year.

Cash Budget for the Period January -- March

	January	February	March
Beginning cash balance	$25,000	_____	_____
Add cash receipts:			
Current month	_____	_____	_____
Prior month	_____	_____	_____
Total receipts	_____	_____	_____
Total cash available	_____	_____	_____
Less cash disbursements:			
Current purchases	_____	_____	_____
Prior purchases	_____	_____	_____
Selling and Administrative costs	_____	_____	_____
Total disbursements	_____	_____	_____
Ending cash balance	_____	_____	_____

Pause and Reflect:

The budgeting process culminates in the cash budget and pro forma financial statements. Pro forma reports are prepared for internal use only. Why aren't these reports distributed to external stakeholders?

_____
_____
_____
_____
_____
_____
_____
_____
_____
_____
_____
_____
_____
_____
_____
_____

Solutions for Chapter 5

Problem 1

1. T	6. T
2. F	7. T
3. T	8. T
4. F	9. F
5. T	10. T

Problem II

1. d
2. a
3. d
4. a
5. a

Problem III

8	Budgeting	17	Normal standard
2	Budgetary slack	12	Padding the budget
9	Direct labor	15	Participative budgeting
13	Direct materials	11	Pro forma financial reports
14	Ideal standard	4	Project budgeting
16	Incremental budgeting	3	Pull system
18	Indirect labor	10	Stockout cost
7	Indirect materials	6	Strategic budget
1	Master budgeting	5	Zero-based budgeting

Problem IV

1. budgeting director
2. Participative
3. evaluate, control
4. nonvalue-added
5. Mandated
6. operational budget
7. sales
8. labor, materials
9. cash

Part V

	January	February	March
Cash Budget for the Period January -- March			
Beginning cash balance	$25,000	$13,800	$31,600
Add cash receipts:			
Current month	$30,000	$42,000	$36,000
Prior month		$20,000	$28,000
Total receipts	$30,000	$62,000	$64,000
Total cash available	$55,000	$75,800	$95,600
Less cash disbursements:			
Current purchases	$31,200	$26,400	$26,400
Prior purchases		$ 7,800	$ 6,600
Selling and Administrative costs	$10,000	$10,000	$10,000
Total disbursements	$41,200	$44,200	$43,000
Ending cash balance	$13,800	$31,600	$52,600

Pause and Reflect

Pro forma financial statements express the goals of management for the period. These reports are based on planned expectations and are used to guide operating decisions. Management does not want external stakeholders to infer that the pro forma reports offer a guarantee of performance outcomes. Therefore, pro forma statements are limited to internal use.

Chapter 6   Short-Term Operating Decisions

Learning Objective 1:

Describe the economic framework for short-term decision making.

Summary

Short-term operating decisions require making choices among alternatives that arise from changed business conditions and that offer opportunities for making more money than originally planned. An understanding of sunk costs, variability of an item having different values across alternatives, and opportunity costs is important for making short-term operating decisions. Incremental analysis forms the economic framework. The steps include: (1) Identify the alternative actions, (2) Determine the incremental effect of each alternative on profit, and (3) Choose the alternative that produces the highest incremental profit.

Learning Objective 2:

Explain how to apply the economic framework to special order decisions.

Summary

The first step is to identify the alternative actions: to accept the special order offer and sell the product, or reject the offer. Second, determine the incremental profit by comparing the relevant revenues and costs of accepting the offer against zero. Third, select the alternative with the higher incremental profit.

Learning Objective 3:

Describe the economic framework for deletion or addition decisions.

Summary

A deletion decision deals with whether to delete a product line that is not as profitable as expected. First, identify the alternatives. Second, calculate the incremental profit. Costs that do not vary across alternatives are irrelevant. The decision rule is to delete a product if it has negative incremental profit or if it can be replaced with a product with higher incremental profit. The addition decision involves an identification of alternatives and determination of incremental profit. The decision rule is to add a product line only if it has a positive incremental profit.

Learning Objective 4:

Use the economic framework to solve make-or-buy problems.

Summary

Manufacturers face the alternatives of making a product or component or buying it from an outside supplier in make-or-buy decisions. Making the product usually results in increased production costs. The first step is to identify the alternatives. Second, determine the incremental profit by identifying all relevant revenues and costs. Opportunity costs may need to be included in the analysis. Select the alternative with the highest incremental profit.

Learning Objective 5:

Apply the economic framework to sell-or-process-further decisions.

Summary

In a sell-or-process-further decision, management must determine whether the incremental revenue is greater than the incremental cost of selling a product at an earlier or a later production stage. The decision rule is: sell the product after further processing if the incremental profit due to further processing is positive.

Learning Objective 6: (Appendix)

Describe how companies use linear programming to determine product mix.

Summary

Linear programming is a mathematical tool used to determine the optimal output given existing scarce resource constraints or limits. The linear programming problem is expressed as mathematical functions and can be solved using the following steps: (1) State the objective function (profit goal), (2) State the constraints (limits on scarce resources), (3) Solve the constraint functions, and (4) Determine the optimal solution. The optimal solution is the one possible solution that produces the highest total contribution margin.

Outline of Key Concepts

I. Using an economic framework for making short-term operating decisions.

    A. Short-term operating decisions--require making choices among alternatives that arise from changes in business circumstances. Short-term decisions differ from other operating decisions.

        1. Based on assumption that current capacity is fixed.

        2. Not planned as part of the management cycle.

        3. Unique.

    B. Decision-relevant variables are quantities, revenues, or costs that differ in one or more alternatives. Begin analysis by asking whether the variable is irrelevant.

        1. Aspects of products that vary but do not have an economic effect on price or quantity are irrelevant and should not be included in economic decisions.

        2. Sunk costs are past costs and do not vary across decision alternatives. Sunk costs ire irrelevant in economic decisions.

        3. Opportunity cost is the foregone benefits of the next best alternative. Is an important concept in short-term decisions.

    C. Incremental analysis is the basis of the economic framework. It answers the question: Which alternative in the opportunity set increases profit the most?

        1. Focuses on the differences among incremental revenues, costs, and profits of the alternatives considered.

        2. Steps in applying incremental analysis include:

            a. Identify the alternative actions. Choosing to do nothing is usually one alternative.

            b. Determine the incremental effect of each alternative on profit:

                i. Find the incremental revenue for each alternative.

ii. Determine the relevant costs for each alternative and calculate the incremental costs for each alternative. Fixed costs do not change in the short run, so they do not vary across alternatives.

iii. Use the difference between the incremental revenue and the incremental costs for each alternative to find the incremental profit.

c. Choose the alternative that produces the highest incremental profit.

II. Applying the economic framework to four types of short-term operating decisions.

A. Special order decisions--company must decide whether to accept a customer's offer to buy the company's product for an amount that is less than the normal selling price.

1. Accepting the special order will increase revenues and costs. Rejecting the special order will leave revenues and costs unchanged.

2. Applying the three steps of the economic framework:

a. Identify the alternative actions--accept the offer and sell the product or reject the offer.

b. Compare the relevant revenues and costs of accepting the offer against zero to determine incremental profit.

c. Choose the alternative with the highest incremental profit.

3. A general economic rule is to accept a special order if the additional revenue generated is greater than the additional costs incurred.

B. Deletion or addition of product lines.

1. Deletion of a product line uses three steps of the economic framework.

a. Identify the alternatives, determine incremental profit, and select the best alternative.

b. Decision rule is to delete a product if it has a negative incremental profit or if it is possible to replace it with a product with higher incremental profit.

2. Addition of a product also uses three steps of the economic framework.

    a. Identify the alternatives, determine the incremental profit, and select the best alternative.

    b. Add a product line only if it has a positive incremental profit.

C. Make-or-buy decisions--manufacturers have the alternatives of making a product or buying it from an outside supplier.

    1. Making the product would increase production costs while buying it would result in increased purchasing costs.

    2. Apply the three steps of the economic framework: Identify the alternatives, identify the relevant revenues and costs to determine incremental profit, and select the best alternative.

    3. Fixed overhead costs are not relevant to the decision

D. Sell-or-process-further decisions--choices between selling a product at an earlier stage of production or processing it further and selling it at a later stage of production.

    1. Incremental revenues--additional revenue per unit if the product is sold after it has been processed further.

    2. Incremental costs--additional costs incurred in processing the product further.

    3. Joint products--two or more separable identifiable products that arise from a common process.

        a. Split-off point--point where the separate products can be identified.

        b. Joint costs--production costs incurred up to the split-off point. They are sunk costs and, therefore, are not relevant to the decision.

    4. Apply the three steps--identify the alternatives, determine incremental profit, and select the best alternative.

    5. The decision rule is to sell the product after further processing if the incremental profit due to further processing is positive.

III. Appendix--Linear Programming: Helping Solve Complex Choices

A. Linear programming--a mathematical tool used to determine the optimal output given existing constraints or limits on scarce resources available.

1. The relevant variables in the problem are expressed in terms of mathematical functions.

2. Linear programming problems can be solved by completing the following steps:

a. State the objective function (profit goal).

i. Maximize the contribution margin of the firm.

b. State the constraints (limits on scarce resources).

c. Solve the constraint functions.

d. Determine the optimal solution (the solution that produces the highest total contribution margin).

Problem I

Indicate whether the following statements are either true (T) or false (F).

_____ 1. Short-term decisions are based on the assumption that business cannot change its plant capacity in the time affected by the decision.
_____ 2. Short-term decisions are planned as a part of the normal management cycle.
_____ 3. Sunk costs will be considered relevant in most short-term operating decisions.
_____ 4. Opportunity costs are irrelevant in the decision-making process.
_____ 5. The first step in incremental analysis is to identify the alternatives.
_____ 6. Fixed costs will have an incremental cost of zero.
_____ 7. Qualitative factors should not be considered in the short-term decision-making process.
_____ 8. Joint product costs are irrelevant in a sell-or-process-further decision.

Problem II

Indicate the correct answer by circling the appropriate answer.

1. Airwest provides a company plane for executives to visit various plants around the world. The company is considering having executives fly commercial rather than use the company plane. Which of the following would be considered a sunk cost in the decision process?
    a. Each flight uses $15,000 in fuel.
    b. Commercial tickets would average $1,500 per flight.
    c. The company plane originally cost 1.5 million.
    d. None of the above are sunk costs.

2. The Weststar company manufactures and sells short-block engines. Budgeted sales and cost data for the year is as follows:

	Total
Sales price	$800,000
Variable costs	450,000
Contribution margin	350,000
Fixed costs	200,000
Net income	$150,000

Budgeted data is based on projected sales of 1,000 engines. Westar has received a special order from a company in Germany for 300 engines at a sales price of $600 each. Westar has the plant capacity to accept the order. If the order is accepted, Westar will incur additional shipping costs of $50 per engine. Fixed costs will remain unchanged. If the order is accepted, the effect on Westar's net income will be an _____.
   a. increase by $35,000
   b. increase by $60,000
   c. increase by $30,000
   d. increase by $105,000

3. Which of the following is not a qualitative factor that must be considered by a manufacturing firm in a make-or-buy decisions?
   a. quality of product
   b. reliability of supplier
   c. employee moral
   d. cost of product

Use the following information for the next two questions:

Dowchem currently manufactures two products in a joint process. If processed further, the following incremental income will result:

Product	Incremental Sales Revenue	Allocated Joint Costs	Additional Processing Costs	Incremental Income
A	$400,000	$125,000	$350,000	<$75,000>
B	$650,000	$140,000	$245,000	$265,000

4. Dowchem can sell product A at splitoff for $20,000. If sold at splitoff, incremental income will
_____.

    a. increase by $20,000
    b. decrease by $50,000
    c. increase by $50,000
    d. decrease by $30,000

5. Dowchem can sell product B at splitoff for $450,000. If sold at splitoff, incremental income will _____.

    a. increase by 450,000
    b. increase by $105,000
    c. increase by $45,000
    d. decrease by $335,000

Problem III

Following is a list of important ideas and key concepts from the chapter. To test your knowledge of these terms, match the term with the definition by placing the number in the space provided.

_____ Incremental cost		_____ Opportunity set	
_____ Joint costs		_____ Split-off point	
_____ Joint products		_____ Sunk costs	
_____ Opportunity costs			

1. The point in the production process where there is identification of separate, saleable products.

2. Two or more separately identifiable products that result from a common production process.

3. A set of costs that do not vary across alternatives; expenditures associated with items already purchased that are irrelevant to future decisions.

4. Costs that cannot be associated specifically with any product because the products are not separately identifiable at the point where the costs were incurred.

5. The change in total cost if one alternative is implemented instead of the other

6. The set of alternatives available to the decision makers from which they will choose the best alternative

7. The forgone benefits of the next best alternative (the one we would have chosen otherwise)

Problem IV

Complete the following sentences by filling in the correct response.

1. Decision relevant variables are _____, _____, or _____ that differ in one or more alternatives.

2. Short-term decisions are _____, _____ operating decisions that were not included as part of planning in the _____ cycle.

3. An _____ framework provides decision makers a way to focus on the _____ variables.

4. Sunk costs are _____ in the decision process.

5. When one alternative is chosen over another, there is an _____ _____ of choosing that alternative.

6. Sound economic decisions require choosing the _____ with the highest _____ _____.

Problem V

1. Fox company currently operates two product lines, A and B. The operating results for the last period are as follows:

	A	B
Sales	$500,000	$400,000
Variable cost of sales	350,000	175,000
Variable selling cost	50,000	25,000
Fixed administrative costs	125,000	125,000
Net income/<loss>	<$ 25,000>	$ 75,000

Fixed administrative costs are allocated equally between product lines. Should product line A be deleted since it does not contribute to overall profitability?

2. Ferris manufacturing, which makes transformers, is operating at full capacity of 10,000 transformers a year. Contribution margin per unit sold is $300. Ferris currently makes the casing but is considering purchasing the part from an outside supplier. Current manufacturing costs include $18 in direct materials, $22 in direct labor and variable overhead, and $10 of allocated fixed overhead. The part will cost $105 each if purchased from an outside supplier. If the part were purchased, 3,000 additional transformers could be produced and sold. Should the company continue to make the casing or purchase it from an outside supplier?

Pause and Reflect:

What qualitative information should a company consider in making the decision about whether to add a product line?

_____
_____
_____
_____
_____
_____
_____
_____
_____
_____
_____
_____
_____
_____
_____
_____

Solutions for Chapter 6

Problem 1

1. T
2. F
3. F
4. F
5. T
6. T
7. F
8. T

Problem II

1. c
2. c
3. d
4. d
5. c

Problem III

5   Incremental cost
4   Joint costs
2   Joint products
7   Opportunity costs

6   Opportunity set
1   Split-off point
3   Sunk costs

Problem IV

1. quantities, revenues, costs
2. short-run, unanticipated, management
3. economic, decision-relevant
4. irrelevant
5. opportunity cost
6. alternative, incremental income

Problem V

1.

	Alternatives		
	A and B	B only	Incremental Change
Sales	$900,000	$400,000	
Variable cost of sales	525,000	175,000	
Variable selling cost	75,000	25,000	
Contribution margin	$300,000	$200,000	<$100,000>

Note: Fixed costs are not included in the analysis because they do not differ between the alternatives.

Fox should keep both product lines. Eliminating product A would result in a $100,000 decrease in net income.

2.

	Alternatives		
Relevant factors	Make	Buy	Incremental Change
Revenues	$ - 0 -	$ 705,000	$ 705,000
Costs:			
Direct materials costs	180,000		180,000
Direct labor and variable overhead	220,000		220,000
Purchase price of casings		1,050,000	<1,050,000>
Income	<$400,000>	<$ 345,000>	$ 55,000

Note: The contribution margin on the 3,000 additional units will only be $235 (($300 - ($105 - $40)) due to the increased cost of the part if purchased. Therefore, the increase in the contribution margin is $705 (3,000 units x $235).

The analysis indicates that Ferris should purchase the casings from the outside supplier. The increased profits due to freed-up capacity more than offset the additional costs paid for the parts.

Pause and Reflect

A company should consider whether the new product line will enhance perceptions about the company's other products or level of quality; whether the product line would provide benefits to customers or society not available otherwise; or whether the product line has any potential for producing negative or hazardous effects.

Chapter 7   Recording and Communicating in the Accounting Cycle

Learning Objective 1:

Use the objectivity principle to explain why financial statements reflect historical cost rather than fair market value and replacement cost.

Summary

The objectivity principle requires that information included in published financial statements must be free of bias. This requires that measurements could be duplicated by independent parties. Fair market value (the sales price that would be agreed upon by unrelated buyers and sellers) requires subjective judgment, which makes it unreliable. Replacement costs (cost of producing or acquiring a similar item) is often subjectively determined. In addition, assets are often replaced with new and improved versions, thus making replacement cost irrelevant. Historical cost (cash or cash equivalent value that either changed hands or became obligated when an accounting event occurred) can be objectively verified. Therefore, the objectivity principle dictates the use of historical cost for external financial statements.

Learning Objective 2:

Understand the revenue recognition and matching principles and their importance.

Summary

The revenue recognition principle states that revenue is recognized and recorded when it is earned. The recognition of a revenue may not coincide with the cash collection. The matching principle requires that all revenues earned during a given period and all expenses incurred in generating those revenues be matched together on the same income statement for the same period. Matching results in a proper measurement of income earned for the period.

Learning Objective 3:

Define accounts and explain the role of debits and credits in a company's accounting system.

Summary

An account accumulates the results of accounting events affecting a particular asset, liability, or owners' equity item. A debit is any dollar amount entered on the left side of an account, and a credit is any amount entered on the right side. For any asset, a debit entry will increase and a credit will decrease the balance of the account. All liability and owners' equity accounts are increased by credit entries and are reduced by debit entries. Revenue accounts are increased by credit entries and decreased by debit entries. Expense accounts are increased by debit entries and decreased by credit entries.

Learning Objective 4:

Explain the flow of accounting events through the accounting system.

Summary

The accounting cycle is the process by which companies record accounting information, transfer it to specific accounts, and assemble it in financial statements. The steps of the accounting cycle are: (1) Identify, analyze, and record events in the general journal, (2) Post general journal entries to the general ledger, (3) Prepare a trial balance, (4) Enter required adjusting entries in the general journal and post them to the general ledger, (5) Prepare an adjusted trial balance, (6) Prepare financial statements, (7) Enter closing entries in the general journal and post to the general ledger, and (8) Prepare a post-closing trial balance.

Learning Objective 5:

Demonstrate an understanding of how companies use adjusting entries as an application of the matching principle.

Summary

Adjusting entries are made to make sure that all revenues earned and expenses incurred during the period have been recorded. Accruals relate to revenues and expenses that have been earned or incurred but have never been recorded. Deferrals relate to cash and other resources that have been collected prior to revenue being earned or cash and other resources that have been paid prior to expenses being incurred. Depreciation expense is the allocation of the cost of long-term assets as an expense to the periods in which the benefits associated with their use help generate revenues.

Learning Objective 6:

Identify how businesses construct financial statements using information contained in the general ledger.

Summary

The adjusted trial balance is used as the information source for the preparation of the financial statements. The income statement is prepared first because net income is needed to complete the statement of stockholders' equity. Next the statement of stockholders' equity is prepared because its ending balanced is needed to complete the balance sheet. The balance sheet is then prepared. The statement of cash flows is prepared last.

Learning Objective 7:

Describe how companies perform the end-of-period closing process and explain the need for the process.

Summary

The closing process involves zeroing out all revenue and expense accounts (nominal accounts) and transferring these balances ultimately to Retained Earnings (a real account). This process is undertaken so that the retained earnings balance reflects the impact of all revenues earned and expenses incurred during the period. The steps of the closing process are: (1) Debit all revenue accounts and transfer their credit balances to the Income Summary account, (2) Credit all expense accounts and transfer their debit balances to the Income Summary account, (3) Transfer the resulting balance in the Income Summary account to the Retained Earnings account.

Outline of Key Concepts

I. There are three fundamental accounting principles: objectivity, revenue recognition, and matching.

    A.   Objectivity principle--information included in published financial statements must be free of bias. Measurements must be subject to duplication by independent parties.

        1.   Fair market value--sales price that would be agreed upon by unrelated buyers and sellers.

            a.   Probably most relevant from external user's perspective, but it cannot be objectively determined.

            b.   Requires subjective judgment which makes it unreliable.

        2.   Replacement cost--cost of producing or acquiring a similar item.

            a.   Amount is often subjectively determined.

            b.   Assets may be replaced by new and improved versions.

        3.   Historical cost--cash or cash equivalent value that either changed hands or became obligated when an accounting event occurred. It represents the cash value of the transaction measured at the date the transaction occurred.

            a.   Can be objectively verified.

            b.   U.S. accountants generally record transactions at historical cost.

    B.   Revenue recognition principle--revenue is recognized and recorded when it is earned.

        1.   Revenues result from the performance of a service or a sale of a product.

        2.   Recognition may not coincide with cash collection.

    C.   Matching principle--all revenues earned during a given period and all expenses incurred to generate those revenues must be matched together on the same income statement for the same period.

        1.   Results in a proper measurement of income earned for the period.

2.   Recognize and record expense at the time a benefit is derived from the use of a product or service, not necessarily at the time of purchase or cash payment.

II. Accounts accumulate the results of accounting events affecting a particular asset, liability, or owners' equity item (which includes revenue and expense).

A.   T-accounts are used as informal representations of accounts in the general ledger. A debit is any amount entered on the left side of the account. A credit is any amount entered on the right side of the account.

B.   Increases and decreases in account balances are reflected as follows:

	Debit	Credit
Assets	Increase	Decrease
Liabilities	Decrease	Increase
Owners' Equity	Decrease	Increase
Revenues	Decrease	Increase
Expenses	Increase	Decrease

C.   In recording transactions, every entry must maintain the equality of the accounting equation, and the total of the debits must equal the total of the credits.

III. The accounting cycle is the formal process by which companies record accounting information, transfer it to specific accounts, and assemble it in financial statements. The steps of the accounting cycle follow.

A.   Identify, analyze, and record events in the general journal.

1.   General journal--chronological record of accounting events.

2.   Each entry shows only the effect of the individual transaction, not account balances.

B. Post general journal entries to the general ledger, the place where all accounts are maintained.

    1. Normal balance of any account is determined by the type of entry that increases the account.

Asset	Debit
Liability	Credit
Owners' Equity	Credit
Revenue	Credit
Expense	Debit

    2. Posting--transferring information from the entries in the general journal to the affected general ledger accounts.

C. Prepare a trial balance which is an internal document that lists the balance of each general ledger account.

    1. Used to determine if the total debits equal total credits.

    2. Does not guarantee that correct accounts have been debited or credited, and does not help discover journal entries that were never made.

D. Enter adjusting entries in the general journal and post them to the general ledger.

    1. Adjusting entries--records revenues earned and expenses incurred during the period that have not yet been recorded. There are three categories.

        a. Accruals--revenues and expenses that have been earned or incurred but have never been recorded.

            i. Accrued revenues--have been earned but not recorded because there has been no cash collection or preparation of an invoice. May arise from passage of time or as a result of an activity. Failure to record would understate assets, revenue, income, and owners' equity.

            ii. Accrued expenses--have been incurred but not recorded because no cash has been paid and no invoice received. Failure to record would understate expenses and liabilities and would overstate income and owners' equity.

b.   Deferrals--relate to cash and other resources that have been collected prior to revenue being earned or cash and other resources that have been paid prior to expenses being incurred.

   i.   Deferred revenues--revenues that are collected before they are earned. Collection creates a liability. Failure to adjust an unearned revenue account understates revenues, income, and owners' equity and overstates liabilities.

   ii.   Deferred expenses--payments are made before the expense has been incurred. Payment creates an asset. Failure to adjust understates expenses and overstates assets, income and owners' equity.

   iii.   Estimated allocations--the cost of long-term assets from which benefits will be derived over a period of years must be allocated as an expense to the periods in which the benefits help generate revenues. For plant and equipment, this allocation is called depreciation expense. The allocation of cost of intangible assets is called amortization expense, and the allocated cost of natural resources is called depletion expense.

E.   Prepare an adjusted trial balance.

   1.   Prepared after adjusting entries are posted to the general ledger.

   2.   Checks for the equality of debits and credits.

F.   Prepare financial statements using the information in the adjusted trial balance.

   1.   Income statement prepared first

   2.   Statement of owners' equity prepared next.

   3.   Balance sheet prepared third.

   4.   Statement of cash flows prepared last.

G.   Enter closing entries in the general journal and post them to the general ledger.

   1.   Real accounts--carry their balances from one period to the next. Includes all the accounts on the balance sheet.

   2.   Nominal accounts--related to only a given period of time and must be closed out before the start of a new period. Includes all revenue and expense accounts.

3. Closing process--zeroing out all revenue and expense account balances.

    a. Transferring these balances ultimately to Retained Earnings.

    b. May use a temporary account, Income Summary, to accumulate revenues and expenses before transferring balance to Retained Earnings.

H. Prepare a post-closing trial balance.

    1. Prepared after closing entries posted to the general ledger. Includes only those real accounts shown on the balance sheet.

    2. Is a last check on the equality of debits and credits.

Problem I

Indicate whether the following statements are either true (T) or false (F).

_____1.   Accuracy of replacement cost information is unaffected by changing technology.
_____2.   An expense should be recorded at the time the business derives a benefit from the use of a product or service.
_____3.   A credit entry to a liability account will increase the balance of the account.
_____4.   Total debits must always equal total credits.
_____5.   The normal balance of an asset is a debit balance.
_____6.   A trial balance insures that the correct accounts have been debited and credited.
_____7.   An accrual is the result of collecting cash prior to revenue being earned or cash paid prior to the expense being incurred.
_____8.   The allocation of the cost of an intangible asset is termed amortization expense.
_____9.   Financial statements are prepared from information provided in the adjusted trial balance.
_____10. All nominal accounts must be closed (zeroed out) at the end of the accounting period.

Problem II

Indicate the correct answer by circling the appropriate letter.

1. John Q. Jones, CPA performs various tax services for clients. When will John record revenues earned in his tax practice?
    a. at the time the service is performed
    b. when the cash is received
    c. when John accepts the client
    d. all of the above are correct

2. A _____ is a chronological record of the accounting events that affect a business.
    a. adjusted trial balance
    b. post-closing trial balance
    c. general ledger
    d. general journal

3. All of the following accounts will be closed at the end of the accounting period except

_____.
    a. rent expense
    b. accumulated depreciation
    c. service fees
    d. dividends

Problem III

The following is a list of important ideas and key concepts from the chapter. To test your knowledge of these terms, match the term with the definition by placing the number in the space provided.

_____ Account	_____ Depreciation expense
_____ Accounting cycle	_____ Fair market value
_____ Accruals	_____ Matching principle
_____ Adjusting entries	_____ Net worth
_____ Amortization expense	_____ Nominal account
_____ Carrying value	_____ Objectivity principle
_____ Credit	_____ Real account
_____ Debit	_____ Replacement cost
_____ Deferrals	_____ Revenue recognition principle
_____ Depletion expense	_____ Trial balance

1. A temporary account relating to a given period of time and closed out before the start of a new period.

2. The cost of an asset less the amount appearing in its associated contra account. Also referred to as *book value* or *undepreciated* cost

3. The accounting principle requiring that all revenues earned during a given period, as well as expenses incurred to earn those revenues, be matched together on the same income statement for the same period.

4. Entries that adjust the amount of accruals, deferrals, and estimated allocations made prior to financial statement preparation

5. The cost of producing or otherwise acquiring an exactly identical item

6. Revenues collected in advance of being earned and expenses paid in advance of being incurred

7. An internal report showing all a company's accounts and their debit or credit balances. It is used to verify the equality of debit and credit account balances

8. The cost of natural resources allocated to the periods benefited

9. The entry made on the left-hand side of an account

10. A permanent account whose balance is carried over from year to year

11. The idea that revenues should be recorded and recognized when the service is performed or the sale has occurred

12. A place to accumulate the results of accounting events affecting particular asset, liability, or owners' equity items. It reflects the increases, decreases, and cumulative balance of the respective items.

13. Revenue and expense events that have taken place but have not been recorded prior to the adjusting process and subsequent financial statement preparation

14. The accounting principle requiring that information included in published financial statements must be free of bias

15. A sales price that would be agreed upon by willing, unrelated buyers and sellers

16. Formal process by which companies record accounting information, transfer it to specific accounts, and assemble it for the preparation of financial statements

17. The cost of intangible assets allocated to the periods benefited

18. The cost of plant assets allocated to the periods benefited, or the portion of an asset's cost which is deducted from revenues of the current period

19. The residual amount left over when total liabilities are subtracted from total assets. It is another way of referring to owners' equity

20. The entry made on the right-hand side of an account

Problem IV

Complete the following sentences by filling in the correct response.

1. Fair market value requires the use of _____ judgment, which renders it _____, and therefore, inappropriate for use in preparation of financial statements.

2. An advantage of _____ cost over other valuation concepts is that it can be objectively verified.

3. Revenue is recognized (recorded) by a company when it is _____.

4. All _____ are maintained in the _____ ledger.

5. The net worth of a business increases when _____ are earned and decreases when _____ are incurred.

6. A _____ _____ insures the equality of debits and credits prior to the preparation of financial statements.

7. Balance sheet accounts are referred to as _____ accounts because their account balances carry over from year to year.

Problem V

For each of the following, indicate whether a debit entry or a credit entry will increase or decrease the balance in the account. The first account is done as an example.

	Increased by	Decreased by
	debit	credit
Land		
Cash	_____	_____
Prepaid insurance	_____	_____
Rent expense	_____	_____
Retained earnings	_____	_____
Capital stock	_____	_____
Supplies	_____	_____
Utilities expense	_____	_____
Inventory	_____	_____
Notes payable	_____	_____
Accumulated depreciation	_____	_____
Patents	_____	_____
Salaries payable	_____	_____

Problem VI

The following events occurred during the first month of operations of Clean-em-up Janitorial Services, Inc. Create and label the T-accounts necessary to record the transactions. Enter the transactions into the T-accounts and prepare an unadjusted trial balance as of the end of the first month of operations. (Use the letters to label the transactions in the T-accounts).

a) Issued capital stock for $50,000.
b) Purchased cleaning supplies for $15,000 on account.
c) Paid $1,500 for the first three months rent on an office building.
d) Paid a $1,200 insurance premium in advance.
e) Purchased cleaning equipment for $8,000 by paying 10% down and issuing a note payable for the balance.
f) Received $4,000 for cleaning services performed.
g) Paid employee's salaries of $1,800.
h) Paid $10,000 of the amount owed for the purchase in (b) above.
i) Billed clients $8,000 for services performed.
j) Paid a $2,000 dividend to owners.

T-Accounts:

Clean-em-up Janitorial Services, Inc.
Unadjusted Trial Balance
End of Month One

	Debit	Credit

Problem VII

The unadjusted trial balance for Rolex, Inc. is presented below, together with information to complete any necessary adjusting entries:

Rolex, Inc.
Unadjusted Trial Balance
December 31, 19X7

	Debits	Credits
Cash..	22,000	
Accounts receivable.......................................	75,000	
Supplies...	9,000	
Prepaid insurance...	12,000	
Equipment..	125,000	
Accumulated depreciation..............................		20,000
Accounts payable..		18,000
Capital stock..		150,000
Retained earnings (balance at beginning of year).......		31,000
Service revenue earned...................................		95,000
Rent expense..	24,000	
Utilities expense...	7,000	
Salaries expense..	32,000	
Miscellaneous expense....................................	8,000	
Totals	314,000	314,000

Adjustment Data:
a) Unused supplies on hand at the end of the year were $2,400.
b) Prepaid insurance consists of a two-year policy paid on July 1, 19X7.
c) Depreciation expense for the year is $5,000.
d) Salaries earned by employees but not paid at year-end were $1,400.

Required: Prepare the adjusting entries for the year in general journal form (you may omit explanations). Prepare T-accounts for the accounts affected by the adjusting entries and post the appropriate amounts. Prepare an adjusted trial balance, an income statement, statement of changes in retained earnings, and a balance sheet.

General Journal

Date	Account Title	Debit	Credit

T-accounts

Rolex, Inc.
Adjusted Trial Balance
December 31, 19X7

	Debit	Credit
————————————	————	————
————————————	————	————
————————————	————	————
————————————	————	————
————————————	————	————
————————————	————	————
————————————	————	————
————————————	————	————
————————————	————	————
————————————	————	————
————————————	————	————
————————————	————	————
————————————	————	————
————————————	————	————
————————————	————	————
————————————	————	————
————————————	————	————
————————————	————	————
————————————	————	————
————————————	————	————
————————————	————	————
————————————	————	————

Rolex, Inc.
Income Statement
For the year ended December 31, 19X7

Rolex, Inc.
Statement of Changes in Retained Earnings
For the year ended December 31, 19X7

Rolex, Inc.
Balance Sheet
December 31, 19X7

Pause and Reflect:

The cost of long-term assets, such as plant and equipment, intangible assets, and natural resources are allocated to expense accounts over the assets' expected useful life. Patents, an intangible asset, have an expected 17-year legal life. Over what period of time should the cost of a patent be amortized or allocated to an expense? Would the amortization period be less than, equal to, or greater than 17 years? Why?

_____
_____
_____
_____
_____
_____
_____
_____
_____
_____
_____
_____
_____
_____
_____
_____
_____
_____
_____
_____
_____

Solutions for Chapter 7

Problem 1

1. F   6. F
2. T   7. F
3. T   8. T
4. T   9. T
5. T   10. T

Problem II

1. a
2. d
3. b

Problem III

12	Account	18	Depreciation expense
16	Accounting cycle	15	Fair market value
13	Accruals	3	Matching principle
4	Adjusting entries	19	Net worth
17	Amortization expense	1	Nominal account
2	Carrying value	14	Objectivity principle
20	Credit	10	Real account
9	Debit	5	Replacement cost
6	Deferrals	11	Revenue recognition principle
8	Depletion expense	7	Trial balance

Problem IV

1. subjective, unreliable
2. historical
3. earned
4. accounts, general
5. revenues, expenses
6. trial balance
7. real (permanent)

Problem V

	Increased by	Decreased by
Land	debit	credit
Cash	debit	credit
Prepaid insurance	debit	credit
Rent expense	debit	credit
Retained earnings	credit	debit
Capital stock	credit	debit
Supplies	debit	credit
Utilities expense	debit	credit
Inventory	debit	credit
Notes payable	credit	debit
Accumulated depreciation	credit	debit
Patents	debit	credit
Salaries payable	credit	debit

Problem VI

Cash				Accounts Receivable		Supplies	
(a)	50,000	(c)	1,500	(i) 8,000		(b) 15,000	
(f)	4,000	(d)	1,200				
		(e)	800				
		(g)	1,800				
		(h)	10,000				
		(j)	2,000				
	36,700						

Prepaid Rent		Prepaid Insurance		Equipment	
(c) 1,500		(d) 1,200		(e) 8,000	

Accounts Payable		Notes Payable		Capital Stock	
(h) 10,000	(b) 15,000		(e) 7,200		(a) 50,000
	5,000				

Dividends		Service Revenue		Salaries Expense	
(j) 2,000			(f) 4,000	(g) 1,800	
			(i) 8,000		
			12,000		

Problem VI (continued)

<table>
<tr><td colspan="3" align="center">**Clean-em-up Janitorial Services, Inc.**
Unadjusted Trial Balance
End of Month One</td></tr>
<tr><td></td><td>**Debit**</td><td>**Credit**</td></tr>
<tr><td>Cash</td><td>36,700</td><td></td></tr>
<tr><td>Accounts receivable</td><td>8,000</td><td></td></tr>
<tr><td>Supplies</td><td>15,000</td><td></td></tr>
<tr><td>Prepaid rent</td><td>1,500</td><td></td></tr>
<tr><td>Prepaid insurance</td><td>1,200</td><td></td></tr>
<tr><td>Equipment</td><td>8,000</td><td></td></tr>
<tr><td>Accounts payable</td><td></td><td>5,000</td></tr>
<tr><td>Notes payable</td><td></td><td>7,200</td></tr>
<tr><td>Capital stock</td><td></td><td>50,000</td></tr>
<tr><td>Dividends</td><td>2,000</td><td></td></tr>
<tr><td>Service revenue</td><td></td><td>12,000</td></tr>
<tr><td>Salaries expense</td><td>1,800</td><td></td></tr>
<tr><td>Totals</td><td>74,200</td><td>74,200</td></tr>
</table>

Problem VII

	General Journal		
Date	*Account Title*	*Debit*	*Credit*
12/31	Supplies expense	6,600	
	Supplies		6,600
12/31	Insurance expense	3,000	
	Prepaid insurance		3,000
12/31	Depreciation expense	5,000	
	Accumulated depreciation		5,000
12/31	Salaries expense	1,400	
	Salaries payable		1,400

Problem VII (continued)

T-accounts

Supplies	
Bal. 9,000	Adj. 6,600
2,400	

Supplies Expense	
Adj. 6,600	

Prepaid Insurance	
Bal. 12,000	Adj. 3,000
9,000	

Insurance Expense	
Adj. 3,000	

Depreciation Expense	
Adj. 5,000	

Accumulated Depreciation	
	Bal. 20,000
	Adj. 5,000
	25,000

Salaries Expense	
Bal. 32,000	
Adj. 1,400	
33,400	

Salaries Payable	
	Adj. 1,400

Rolex, Inc.
Adjusted Trial Balance
December 31, 19X7

	Debit	Credit
Cash..	22,000	
Accounts receivable......................................	75,000	
Supplies..	2,400	
Prepaid insurance..	9,000	
Equipment..	125,000	
Accumulated depreciation...............................		25,000
Accounts payable...		18,000
Salaries payable..		1,400
Capital stock...		150,000
Retained earnings (balance at beginning of year).......		31,000
Service revenue earned...................................		95,000
Rent expense...	24,000	
Utilities expense..	7,000	
Salaries expense..	33,400	
Miscellaneous expense....................................	8,000	
Supplies expense..	6,600	
Insurance expense...	3,000	
Depreciation expense......................................	5,000	
Totals	320,400	320,400

Problem VII (continued)

Rolex, Inc.
Income Statement
For the year ended December 31, 19X7

Revenues:		
Service revenue earned		$95,000
Expenses:		
Rent expense	$24,000	
Utilities expense	7,000	
Salaries expense	33,400	
Miscellaneous expense	8,000	
Supplies expense	6,600	
Insurance expense	3,000	
Depreciation expense	5,000	87,000
Net Income		8,000

Rolex, Inc.
Statement of Changes in Retained Earnings
For the year ended December 31, 19X7

Beginning balance	$31,000
Add: Net income	8,000
Deduct: Dividends paid	- 0 -
Ending balance	$39,000

Problem VII (continued)

Rolex, Inc.
Balance Sheet
As of December 31, 19X7

Assets

Current assets:		
Cash		$ 22,000
Accounts receivable		75,000
Supplies		2,400
Prepaid insurance		9,000
Total current assets		$108,400
Long-term assets:		
Equipment	$125,000	
Less: Accumulated depreciation	25,000	$100,000
Total assets		$208,400

Liabilities

Current liabilities:		
Accounts payable		$ 18,000
Salaries payable		1,400
Total current liabilities		$ 19,400

Stockholders' Equity

Capital stock	$150,000	
Retained earnings	39,000	189,000
Total liabilities and stockholders' equity		$208,400

Pause and Reflect:

Patents have a legal life of 17 years, but most patents provide economic benefits to a company for a much shorter period of time. For example, in the information technology industry, improvements in hardware occur so quickly that "state-of-the-art" equipment becomes obsolete in two to three years. Therefore, patents must be amortized over the period of time from which economic benefits will be derived. Thus, most patents will be amortized over a period of less than 17 years. The amortization period cannot exceed the legal life of the patent, which is 17 years.

Chapter 8   Recording and Communicating
in the Expenditure Cycle

Learning Objective 1:

Explain the differences among expense, expenditure, and loss and the distinction between inventoriable and noninventoriable cost.

Summary

An expense is a decrease in assets or increase in liabilities and a decrease in owners' equity due to the operations of a business. A loss is a decrease in assets or increase in liabilities and a decrease in owners' equity arising from events incidental to the operations of the business. Expenditures are cash payments made to acquire goods or services, pay liabilities, or pay owners a return on their investment. Inventoriable cost is the cost incurred to acquire merchandise for resale, while noninventoriable cost is the cost of goods and services that support the sale of the firm's goods and services.

Learning Objective 2:

Describe how to record events involving the purchase and use of noninventoriable goods and services in the expenditure cycle.

Summary

The consumption of noninventoriable goods and services requires the recording of an operating expense which matches the expense with the revenues generated during the period. The expense may be recognized at the time of the cash expenditure, after goods and services are acquired, or before the time of the cash expenditure. Noninventoriable goods and services may be acquired externally, such as advertising; or they may be acquired internally, such as labor.

Learning Objective 3:

Indicate how to record events involving the purchase of inventory in the expenditure cycle.

Summary

Merchandise inventory is recorded in the accounts at the cash or cash equivalent amount at the time of purchase. The purchase price includes any additional costs incurred to obtain the inventory, such as transportation costs or insurance. The purchase price may be reduced by purchase discounts or purchase returns and allowances. The inventory may be recorded using either a periodic inventory system or a perpetual inventory system.

Learning Objective 4:

Explain the difference between the FIFO and LIFO cost flow assumptions.

Summary

The first-in, first-out (FIFO) cost flow assumption means that the first inventory costs recorded are the first costs expensed to Cost of Goods Sold and the remaining inventory balance consists of the most recent costs. The last-in, first-out (LIFO) cost flow assumption means that the last inventory costs recorded are the first costs expensed to Cost of Goods Sold, and the inventory balance consists of the oldest inventory costs.

Learning Objective 5:

Describe the relationship between operating expenses and cash expenditures.

Summary

Expenses reflect the outflow of a firm's resources, but they do not describe actual cash outflows. Operating expenses that are associated with prepaid assets or accrued liabilities must be adjusted by the beginning and ending asset or liability account balances to determine the cash expenditures. Operating expenses that are not associated with balance sheet accounts are assumed to equal the cash expenditure for the period.

Learning Objective 6:

Explain how the financial effects of the purchase and use of goods and services are communicated to external and internal users.

Summary

The financial effect of the purchase and use of goods and services is communicated to external users via the financial statements--income statement, balance sheet, and statement of cash flows. The effects are reported to internal users through reports, such as payroll reports and inventory reports.

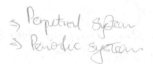

Outline of Key Concepts

I. Introduction to the expenditure cycle.

    A. Merchandise inventory--goods that a merchandising company acquires with the intent of selling.

        1. Recorded as an asset at time of purchase.

        2. Transferred into the expense account Cost of Goods Sold when sold.

    B. Noninventoriable goods and services--goods and services that support the sale of the firm's goods and services.

        1. Classified as operating expenses once they are consumed.

II. Understanding the differences among expenditure, expense, and loss.

    A. Expenditures--cash payments made to acquire goods and services, reduce liabilities, or reward owners for their interest in the firm.

    B. Expense--a decrease in assets or increase in liabilities and a decrease in owners' equity resulting from the operations of the business.

    C. Loss--a decrease in assets or increases in liabilities and a decrease in owners' equity resulting from events that are incidental to the ongoing operations of the firm.

III. Accounting for noninventoriable goods and services acquired externally or internally.

    A. Accounting for external operating expenditures and expenses.

        1. Expense recognized at the time of the cash expenditure.

        2. Expense recognized after goods and services are acquired.

            a. Examples include prepaid insurance and office supplies.

            b. As goods or services are used, the asset account is reduced and the expense is recognized.

        3. Expense recognized before the time of the cash expenditure (accrued expenses). Warranties and income taxes are examples.

B. Accounting for internal operating expenditures and expenses: payroll.

1. Important terms include gross pay (amount earned), deductions (amounts withheld by the employer), and net pay (amount remaining after deductions are subtracted from gross pay).

2. Withholdings may be mandated or voluntary.

   a. Mandated withholdings include federal income taxes, FICA taxes, and perhaps state and local income taxes.

   b. Voluntary withholdings include pensions, life insurance, charitable contributions, union dues, etc.

   c. Deductions become liabilities to the employer at the time they are withheld. Employer must pay these deductions to another organization on behalf of the employee.

   d. Wages expense is equal to the gross pay and wages payable is equal to net pay.

3. Employer must pay payroll taxes.

   a. Must pay a portion of an employee's social security taxes (FICA taxes) and unemployment taxes on the salaries and wages of employees.

   b. Use one expense account, Payroll Tax Expense but separate liability accounts because the liabilities must be paid to different government agencies.

IV. Accounting for the acquisition of merchandise inventory is at the cash or cash equivalent amount at the time of the purchase.

A. Cost of merchandise inventory includes the purchase price plus additional costs incurred to obtain the inventory, such as freight-in and insurance charges.

1. FOB destination means the seller is responsible for freight and insurance charges while FOB shipping point means the buyer is responsible for freight and insurance.

2. Purchase discounts--cash discount taken which results in the buyer paying less than the original amount due.

Introduction to Accounting: An Integrated Approach, 1st Edition

      a.   Net price method--assumes all purchase discounts taken. Cost of merchandise inventory is purchase price less any cash discount.

      b.   Purchase discounts lost--considered a financing charge to the buyer.

  3.   Purchase returns and allowances--buyer's obligation to the seller and the cost of inventory are reduced because either merchandise is returned to the seller or a price adjustment has been made on the purchase.

B.   Periodic versus perpetual inventory systems.

  1.   Periodic inventory system--recording system that reflects the cost of goods sold and inventory quantities only at periodic intervals.

  2.   Perpetual inventory system--purchasing company maintains a continual record of the quantity and cost of inventory items purchased and sold. All events that increase or decrease inventory quantities or cost are recorded directly into the inventory account.

V. Cost flow assumptions are rational and systematic allocations of inventory cost between Cost of Goods Sold and Inventory.

A.   Specific Identification--each item of inventory has an identification code that enables management to monitor the status of each item.

B.   First-in, first-out (FIFO) cost flow assumption--first inventory costs recorded are the first costs expensed to Cost of Goods Sold. Remaining inventory balance consists of the most recent costs.

  1.   FIFO approximates the physical flow of goods.

  2.   In periods of rising prices, FIFO results in the older, lower prices appearing on the income statement and the newer, higher prices appearing on the balance sheet.

C.   Last-in, first-out (LIFO) cost flow assumption--last inventory costs recorded are the first costs expensed to Cost of Goods Sold. The inventory balance consists of the oldest inventory costs.

  1.   In periods of rising prices, LIFO results in the newer, higher prices appearing on the income statement and the older, lower prices appearing on the balance sheet.

      a.   Although lower income results, a company may choose to adopt LIFO because the lower income results in a lower income tax expense.

b.   If LIFO is used for tax purposes, it must be used for financial statement reporting purposes as well.

VI. Reporting operating events to external and internal users.

A.   Information is reported to external users via the financial statements.

1.   Multistep income statement--list cost of goods sold separately from other expenses. Cost of goods sold is subtracted from sales to derive gross margin. See Exhibit 8.8.

2.   Balance sheet--reports the assets and liabilities associated with the purchase and use of goods and services.

a.   Must disclose the cost flow assumption used.

b.   Must report the market value of inventory if it is less than the cost of the inventory.

3.   Statement of cash flows--shows the cash flows expended to generate the revenues for the same period.

a.   Liquidity--time which is required to convert an asset into cash or use it in operations.

b.   Determining cash expenditure identified with a particular expense and prepaid account: expense for the period plus the ending balance in the prepaid account minus the beginning balance of the prepaid account.

c.   Determining cash expenditure identified with accrued liabilities and a particular expense: expense for the period plus the beginning balance of the liability account minus the ending liability account balance.

d.   Other operating expenses not associated with a balance sheet account are assumed to equal the cash expenditure for the period.

e.   Determining the amount of cash paid for inventory: Cost of goods sold plus the ending balance in inventory account minus the beginning balance in inventory account equals inventory purchased during the period. Then add the beginning balance in accounts payable to the purchases and subtract the ending balance of accounts payable.

B. Information is reported to internal users in reports that vary in level of detail and frequency.

    1. Examples of specialized reports are payroll reports and inventory reports. See Exhibits 8.11 and 8.12.

VII. Financial statements can be subject to distortion and misinterpretation.

A. Errors in accounting for noninventoriable goods and services.

    1. Cutoff error--failure to make an appropriate adjusting entry which results in the failure to recognize the appropriate amount of expense for a particular period.

B. Distortions created by inventory errors.

    1. If ending inventory is overstated, net income is overstated because cost of goods sold is understated.

    2. If ending inventory is understated, net income is understated because cost of goods sold is overstated.

C. Use of LIFO cost flow assumption results in realistic reported income but in understated assets on the balance sheet when prices are rising. FIFO results in a realistic balance sheet but overstatement of income when prices are rising.

Problem I

Indicate whether the following statements are either true (T) or false (F).

_____1.   Office supplies would be considered a noninventoriable good.
_____2.   A payment of a dividend to stockholders would be considered an expense.
_____3.   Taxable income is calculated by a corporation using generally accepted accounting principles.
_____4.   Deductions from gross pay become a liability of the employer at the time they are withheld.
_____5.   Shipping charges (FOB shipping point) will not be included in the cost of a company's inventory.
_____6.   Purchases discounts lost will increase the cost of inventory included on the balance sheet.
_____7.   A periodic inventory system is used by companies that are capable of keeping a running balance of the cost of goods available for sale and cost of goods sold during a period.
_____8.   The LIFO cost assumption reflects that costs are charged to cost of goods sold in reverse chronological order.
_____9.   In periods of rising prices, the use of a LIFO cost flow assumption will result in a lower net income than FIFO.

Problem II

Indicate the correct answer by circling the appropriate letter.

Use the following information for the next two questions:

Ontech sells optical readers under a 5-year warranty. Ontech estimates that 5 percent of the readers will require warranty work and repair costs will average $75 per repair. During the year, 4,000 optical readers were sold and Ontech paid an independent repair company $2,500 for warranty repairs.

1. What amount will Ontech report as warranty expense for the year?
    a. $2,500
    b. $6,500
    c. $15,000
    d. $30,000

2. Assume the Estimated Warranty Liability account had a $1,800 credit balance at the beginning of the year. What is the balance in the account at the end of the year?
    a. $1,800
    b. $2,500
    c. $15,000
    d. $14,300

3. Which of the following is not a payroll tax levied against the employer?
    a. FICA
    b. FUTA
    c. SUTA
    d. all are payroll taxes levied against the employer

4. Amtech uses a perpetual inventory system and the net price method to account for its inventory. Amtech purchased 2,000 items of inventory at a price of $5 each. Terms of the sale were 2/10,n30, FOB shipping point. Shipping charges were $500. Due to an oversight in the accounting department, the invoice was not paid within the discount period. As a result of the above transactions, the inventory account will increase by _____.
    a. $9,800
    b. $10,000
    c. $10,300
    d. $10,500

5. Lex Corp. reported salaries expense of $125,000 on the 19X7 income statement. Salaries payable had a beginning balance of $4,000 and an ending balance of $3,000. What amount will be shown on the cash flow statement for payment of salaries?
   a. $125,000
   b. $129,000
   c. $126,000
   d. $124,000

Use the following information for the next three questions:

The following is a chronological record of inventory events for the first month of operations. A perpetual inventory system is used:

	Number of units		Unit	Total
	Bought	Sold	Price	Cost
Purchase	400		$2.00	$800
Sale		300		
Purchase	200		$2.50	$500
Purchase	300		$3.00	$900
Sale		400		

6. If a FIFO cost flow assumption is used, ending inventory shown on the balance sheet will be

   _____.
   a. $400
   b. $600
   c. $550
   d. $660

7. If a LIFO cost flow assumption is used, ending inventory shown on the balance sheet will be

   _____.
   a. $400
   b. $350
   c. $450
   d. $600

8. If a LIFO cost flow assumption is used, cost of goods sold reported on the income statement will be _____.
   a. $1,750
   b. $1,900
   c. $2,100
   d. $1,550

9. Milex reported rent expense of $18,000 on the 19X7 income statement. Prepaid rent had a beginning balance of $2,000 and an ending balance of $8,000. What amount will be shown on the cash flow statement for payment of rent?

    a. $18,000

    b. $8,000

    c. $12,000

    d. $24,000

Problem III

The following is a list of important ideas and key concepts from the chapter. To test your knowledge of these terms, match the term with the definition by placing the number in the space provided.

_____ Cost flow assumptions	_____ Net price method
_____ Expenditure	_____ Noninventoriable goods and services
_____ FIFO	_____ Periodic Inventory system
_____ Freight out	_____ Perpetual Inventory system
_____ LIFO	_____ Purchase Discounts Lost
_____ Liquidity	_____ Specific Identification method
_____ Loss	

1. An inventory method that transfers the cost of inventory to Cost of goods Sold when the items that are individually identified are sold

2. The rational and systematic allocation of inventory cost between Cost of goods sold and Inventory by making assumptions about the order in which inventory is sold

3. A method of recording the acquisition of inventory that assumes that the cost of merchandise inventory is the purchase price less any available cash discount

4. A recording system that reflects inventory quantities and cost at the end of the accounting period

5. A decrease in assets or increase in liabilities (net assets) and a decrease in owners' equity resulting from events that are incidental to the ongoing operations of the firm, with the exception of distributions to owners.

6. An account used with the net price method of inventory to record the finance charge for not taking an available discount

7. Cash payment made to acquire goods and services, reduce liabilities, and reward owners for their interest in the firm

8. A recording system that creates a continuous record of the quantity and cost of inventory items purchased and sold

9. Goods and services that support the sale of the firm's goods and services but are not included in the Cost of Goods sold or the merchandise inventory

10. The cost of shipping goods paid by the seller; classified as an operating expense

11. A cost flow assumption that presumes that inventory purchases (costs) are charged to Cost of Goods Sold in chronological order

12. The time required to convert an asset into cash or use it in operations.

13. A cost flow assumption that presumes inventory purchases (costs) are charged to Cost of Goods Sold in reverse chronological order

Problem IV

Complete the following sentences by filling in the correct response.

1. When a company sells its _____, the cost of the items sold is transferred to an expense account called _____.

2. _____ describe events that reduce net assets as goods and services are consumed in normal operations, whereas _____ describe events that are incidental to the firm's operations.

3. Take-home pay is the amount remaining after subtracting _____ from an employee's _____ pay.

4. Under a _____ inventory system, cost of goods sold is recorded at the time of sale.

5. The _____ cost flow assumption means that costs are charged to _____ in chronological order.

6. If ending inventory is understated, net income will be _____ and cost of goods sold will be _____.

7. _____ refers to the time it takes to convert an asset into cash or use it in operations.

Problem V

The following is a chronological record of inventory events for Extar Corporation:

Date		Number of units Bought	Number of units Sold	Unit Price	Total Cost
1/1	Beginning inventory	1,000		$50	$50,000
1/5	Sale		500		
1/12	Purchase	300		$55	$16,500
1/21	Purchase	600		$57	$34,200
1/28	Sale		1,200		

Extar maintains a Perpetual FIFO inventory system. The sales price of Extar's product is $100 per unit and all sales and purchases are made on account.

Required: Prepare the journal entries in general journal form for the month of January (you may omit journal entry descriptions).

General Journal

Date	Account Title	Debit	Credit

Pause and Reflect:

Companies in the consumer goods industry often use premiums (return cards or coupons for free gifts) as incentives to encourage customers to purchase their products. Premiums are usually attached to goods sold to customers. When should companies recognize the expense that is associated with premiums? At the time the premiums are issued? When the premiums are redeemed? Explain.

_____
_____
_____
_____
_____
_____
_____
_____
_____
_____
_____
_____
_____
_____
_____

Solutions for Chapter 8

Problem 1

1. T	6. F
2. F	7. F
3. F	8. T
4. T	9. T
5. F	

Problem II

1. c
2. d
3. d
4. c
5. c
6. b
7. c
8. a
9. d

Problem III

2	Cost flow assumptions	3	Net price method
7	Expenditure	9	Noninventoriable goods and services
11	FIFO	4	Periodic Inventory system
10	Freight out	8	Perpetual Inventory system
13	LIFO	6	Purchase Discounts Lost
12	Liquidity	1	Specific Identification method
5	Loss		

Problem IV

1. inventory, cost of goods sold
2. expenses, losses
3. deductions, gross
4. perpetual
5. FIFO, cost of goods sold
6. understated, overstated
7. Liquidity

Problem V

	General Journal		
Date	Account Title	Debit	Credit
1/5	Accounts receivable	$50,000	
	Sales		$50,000
	Cost of goods sold	$25,000	
	Inventory		$25,000
1/12	Inventory	$16,500	
	Accounts payable		$16,500
1/21	Inventory	$34,200	
	Accounts payable		$34,200
1/28	Accounts receivable	$120,000	
	Sales		$120,000
	Cost of goods sold	$64,300	
	Inventory		$64,300

Pause and Reflect:

The matching principle requires that the premium expense be recognized at the time of issuance of the premium (sale of the product to which the premium is attached). It is necessary to match the premium cost with the revenue generated by the related sale. Obviously, not all of the premium coupons will be redeemed. Therefore, an estimate of the cost of the premiums redeemed must be made. Thus, at the time of redemption, the liability would be satisfied.

Chapter 9   Recording and Communicating
in the Revenue Cycle

Learning Objective 1:

Understand how to distinguish between revenues and gains.

Summary

Revenues increase the net worth of a business as a result of selling goods or services in the course of the business's ongoing major or central operations. Gains also increase the net worth of a business, but they arise from peripheral or incidental transactions. Both revenues and gains are recognized when they have been earned and realized.

Learning Objective 2:

Explain how the accounting system captures information concerning revenues, gains, and related events, including uncollectible accounts.

Summary

Revenues can be recorded (recognized): (1) at the time cash is collected, (2) before cash is collected, or (3) after cash is collected. The amount of revenue recognized is equal to the cash received or the cash equivalent value of the increase in the net worth resulting from the transaction. Revenues may be reduced by sales returns and allowances and sales discounts. Uncollectible accounts are recorded to achieve proper income measurement and proper asset valuation.

Learning Objective 3:

Describe how companies communicate the financial effects of revenues, gains, and related events to their external and internal stakeholders.

Summary

Companies report revenues and gains through multi-step or single-step income statements. The balance sheet reports the accounts receivable and notes receivable accounts affected by revenue and gain transactions. The statement of cash flows reports the amount of cash receipts from customers during a particular period. Special reports and subsidiary ledgers are used to communicate the financial effects of revenue and gain transactions to internal stakeholders.

Outline of Key Concepts

I. Distinguishing between revenues and gains.

    A.   FASB *Statement of Financial Accounting Concepts, No. 6* defines revenues as "Inflows or other enhancements of assets of an entity or settlements of its liabilities (or a combination of both) from delivering or producing goods, rendering services, or other activities that constitute the entity's ongoing major or central operations."

        1.   Always increase the net worth of a business.

        2.   Result from an earnings process.

        3.   Result from activities that are ongoing and central to operations.

    B.   The FASB defines gains as the increase in net worth resulting from "peripheral or incidental transactions."

    C.   Revenues and gains are recognized when they have been earned and realized.

        1.   Typically, revenues are earned when a company sells a product or renders services to a customer.

        2.   Revenues are realized when an exchange has taken place that yields cash, a claim to cash, or a claim to some other right that results in increased net worth.

        3.   Amount of revenue recognized is equal to the dollar amount of cash received or the cash equivalent value of the increase in net worth resulting from the transaction.

II. Recording revenues, gains, and related transactions.

    A.   Revenue can be recognized at three points.

        1.   At the same time cash is collected--a company performs a service or sells a product and immediately collects cash.

        2.   Before cash is collected.

            a.   Sales on account--record an account receivable.

b. Sales involving promissory notes.

    i. The note is an unconditional written promise to pay a fixed sum of money (principal) plus interest on the principal, on or before a specified future date (maturity date).

    ii. Interest is not part of the sale price but a payment for the use of money.

3. After cash is collected--realization precedes the earnings process. The customer payment creates a liability (unearned revenue) for the business to perform a service or deliver a product in the future.

B. Sales returns and allowances--occurs when a customer is not satisfied with a product or service. The customer may be allowed to return the merchandise or be allowed to pay a reduced price.

1. The event is recorded by debiting a contra-revenue account called sales returns and allowances. The credit is generally to accounts receivable.

C. Sales discounts--a cash discount offered to customers when payment is made within a specified period.

1. Record as a debit to the contra-revenue account sales discounts and as a credit to accounts receivable.

D. Uncollectible accounts from an external user's perspective.

1. Two primary objectives:

a. Proper income measurement--Matching requires that companies estimate the portion of the current year's credit sales that will prove uncollectible and deduct the estimated expense on the income statement.

b. Proper asset valuation--Net realizable value--net dollar amount the company expects to eventually collect after making allowances for estimated uncollectible accounts.

2. Estimated bad debts is recorded by debiting Uncollectible Accounts Expense and crediting a contra-asset account, Allowance for Doubtful Accounts.

a.   The write-off of a specific account is recorded by debiting Allowance for Doubtful Accounts and crediting Accounts Receivable.

b.   The write-off of an account does not change the net realizable value of accounts receivable.

3.   Two basic methods for estimating uncollectible accounts expense exist.

a.   Income statement approach--the expense is based on the historical relationship between credit sales and uncollectible accounts.

b.   Balance sheet approach--estimates the uncollectible portion of account receivables balance.

i.   Aging schedule--group accounts by age. Older receivables are less likely to be collected.

E.   Common source of a gain is the disposal of an income-producing asset. Gain is the difference between the cash or cash equivalent value received and the carrying value of the asset.

III. External reporting of revenues, gains, and related events.

A.   Income statement reports net revenues and gains.

1.   Multistep income statement--reports the calculation of net income in several steps. See Exhibit 9.2.

a.   Report gross margin, separate categories for selling and administrative expenses, separate section for other income (which includes gains).

2.   Single-step income statement--net income is calculated in one step. See Exhibit 9.2.

B.   Balance sheet reports the net realizable value of accounts receivable and the amount of liabilities associated with unearned revenues.

C.   Statement of cash flows reports the amount of cash receipts collected from customers for a particular period.

1. Cash receipts from customers equal net sales for the year plus beginning accounts receivable balance minus ending accounts receivable balance minus beginning of year customer deposits plus end of year customer deposits.

IV. Internal reporting of revenues, gains, and related events.

    A. Detailed sales reports, sales returns and allowances reports, credit reports.

    B. Subsidiary accounts receivable ledger--lists separate account receivables balances.

V. Potential errors in reporting gains and losses.

    A. May be incentives to overstate or understate revenues and gains--improvement in stockholder assessment of performance or reduced taxes.

    B. Most errors are unintentional and often result from improper cutoffs.

Problem I

Indicate whether the following statements are either true (T) or false (F).

_____1. Revenues will always increase the net worth of a business.
_____2. All increases in the net worth of a business are the result of the generation of revenues.
_____3. Gains are profits generated from activities that are central to the operations of the business.
_____4. Revenues are earned when the product is sold or the service has been rendered to a customer.
_____5. Gains are recorded when the cash is received.
_____6. Payment of a promissory note is due on the maturity date.
_____7. Unearned revenue is considered a liability account.
_____8. An increase in the sales discounts account will cause an increase in a company's reported net sales.
_____9. The income statement approach to estimating uncollectible accounts is based on an aging of the end-of-year accounts receivable balance.
_____10. Cash received from the sale of operating assets will be shown in the investments section of the cash flow statement.

Problem II

Indicate the correct answer by circling the appropriate letter.

1. Ferris, Inc. accepted a $10,000, 10 percent, 90-day promissory note in full payment of an accounts receivable balance from a customer. What amount will Ferris receive on the maturity date and by what amount will net worth increase on that date?

	Amount received	Increase in net worth
a.	$10,000	$10,000
b.	$10,247	$10,247
c.	$10,247	$ 247
d.	$10,000	- 0 -

2. On December 31, 19X7, Beltway leasing received a $12,000 payment from a customer for rent on a building for 19X8. Beltway's entry to record receipt of the payment will be _____.

a. Cash	$12,000	
Unearned rental revenue		$12,000
b. Cash	$12,000	
Rental revenue		$12,000
c. Cash	$ 1,000	
Rental revenue		$ 1,000
d. Unearned rental revenue	$12,000	
Cash		$12,000

Use the following information for the next two questions:

The X Company prepared the following summary of its aged accounts receivable as of the last day of the accounting year:

	Receivable Amount	Estimated Percentage Uncollectible
Net yet due	$400,000	1%
1-30 days overdue	100,000	3%
31-90 days overdue	75,000	10%
Over 90 days overdue	50,000	20%
	$625,000	

Allowance for Doubtful Accounts had a credit balance of $1,000 prior to any adjusting entry.

3. What amount will X Company show on its income statement for Uncollectible Accounts Expense?
    a. $200
    b. $23,500
    c. $24,500
    d. $25,500

4. What amount will X Company show on its balance sheet as net realizable value from accounts receivable?
    a. $24,500
    b. $600,500
    c. $625,000
    d. $400,000

5. Y Company reported $400,000 in net sales in 19X7. Accounts receivable had a $60,000 balance at the beginning of the year and a $40,000 balance at the end of the year. What will Y Company report as cash received from customers on its 19X7 cash flow statement?
    a. $400,000
    b. $420,000
    c. $380,000
    d. $460,000

6. Z Company reported $250,000 in salaries expense in 19X7. Salaries payable had a $15,000 balance at the beginning of the year and a $21,000 balance at the end of the year. What will Y Company report as cash paid for salaries on its 19X7 cash flow statement?
    a. $250,000
    b. $265,000
    c. $244,000
    d. $271,000

Problem III

The following is a list of important ideas and key concepts from the chapter. To test your knowledge of these terms, match the term with the definition by placing the number in the space provided.

_____ Aging schedule   _____ Maturity date
_____ Balance sheet approach   _____ Net realizable value
_____ Contra-revenue account   _____ Promissory note
_____ Gains   _____ Revenues
_____ Income statement approach   _____ Subsidiary accounts receivable ledger
_____ Issue date

1. An unconditional written promise to pay a fixed future sum of money, called principal, plus interest on or before a certain date

2. A method of estimating uncollectible accounts expense based upon an analysis of sales activity

3. An account whose balance is deducted from related revenue account. Examples are Sales Discounts and Sales Returns and Allowances

4. A listing of a company's accounts receivable balances grouped by the period of time they have been outstanding

5. The date a promissory note is signed

6. A data storage device listing separate accounts receivable balances, as well as all credit sales and payment activity, for each credit customer

7. The portion of the gross accounts receivable balance that a company estimates it will collect

8. A method of estimating uncollectible accounts expense based upon an analysis of outstanding accounts receivable balances

9. Increases in net worth of a business resulting from an earnings process involving peripheral or incidental transactions

10. The date by which a promissory note must be paid

11. Increases in net worth resulting from an earnings process involving the central, ongoing activity of a business

---

Problem IV

Prepare journal entries in general journal form to record the following selected transactions for the Ace Company. A perpetual inventory system is used.

June 1   Merchandise, which originally cost Ace Company $2,000, is sold for $3,500.

June 5   Merchandise, which originally cost Ace Company $5,000, is sold for $11,000. Terms of the sale are 1/15, n/60 from the sales date.

June 10 Ace Company received a $20,000 deposit on a special order for an overseas customer. Shipment of the merchandise is expected to be made in July.

June 15 A $500 sale to Hexway Inc. is written-off as uncollectible.

June 19 Merchandise, which originally cost Ace Company $1,000, is sold for $2,100. Terms of the sale are 1/15, n/60 from the sales date.

June 20 Payment is received for the June 5th sale (within the discount period).

June 28 $200 of the merchandise sold on June 19th is returned as defective.

June 30 Ace Company received a $4,000 payment from a credit sale made to a customer in May.

General Journal

Date	Account Title	Debit	Credit

General Journal

Date	Account Title	Debit	Credit

Pause and Reflect:

After repeated efforts to collect a customer's account, a company wrote off the account as uncollectible. Subsequently, the account was collected, and the appropriate entries were made. What would these entries be? Would the company grant credit to this customer in the future?

Entries:

Solutions for Chapter 9

Problem 1

1. T		6. T	
2. F		7. T	
3. F		8. F	
4. T		9. F	
5. F		10. T	

Problem II

1. c
2. a
3. b
4. b
5. b
6. c

Problem III

4	Aging schedule	10	Maturity date
8	Balance sheet approach	7	Net realizable value
3	Contra-revenue account	1	Promissory note
9	Gains	11	Revenues
2	Income statement approach	6	Subsidiary accounts receivable ledger
5	Issue date		

Problem IV

Date	Account Title	Debit	Credit
	General Journal		
6/1	Cash	3,500	
	Sales		3,500
	Cost of goods sold	2,000	
	Inventory		2,000
6/5	Accounts receivable	11,000	
	Sales		11,000
	Cost of goods sold	5,000	
	Inventory		5,000
6/10	Cash	20,000	
	Deposit		20,000
6/15	Allowance for doubtful accounts	500	
	Accounts receivable		500
6/19	Accounts receivable	2,100	
	Sales		2,100
	Cost of goods sold	1,000	
	Inventory		1,000
6/20	Cash	10,890	
	Sales discounts	110	
	Accounts receivable		11,000
6/28	Sales returns and allowances	200	
	Accounts receivable		200
6/30	Cash	4,000	
	Accounts receivable		4,000

Pause and Reflect:

The entries to record the subsequent collection of an account that had been written off would be:

Accounts receivable	xx	
Allowance for doubtful accounts		xx
Cash	xx	
Accounts receivable		xx

The company would review the complete credit history of the customer's account and try to determine the reason(s) for the customer's delinquent payment. In addition, the company would analyze the customer's short-term and long-term profitability and cash flow potentials. This analysis would include a review of the customer's sales potential, its competitive position, its credit and collection policies, its current and long-term debt position, and whether its management leadership has changed. It is, therefore, possible that a company may again grant credit to a customer whose account had once been written off as uncollectible.

Chapter 10 Recording and Communicating in the Conversion Cycle

Learning Objective 1:

Explain why cost accumulation is important during the conversion cycle.

Summary

Cost accumulation is important for manufacturing processes for four primary reasons: (1) to determine the cost of products, (2) to determine if the selling prices for products were appropriate to achieve the company's goals, (3) to determine if the mix of products produced and sold was appropriate to achieve the company's goals, and (4) to determine the cost of goods sold for the period.

Learning Objective 2:

Indicate how companies analyze and record material- and labor-related events during the conversion cycle.

Summary

The acquisition cost of raw materials is recorded as Raw Materials Inventory. When raw materials are requisitioned for use in production, the cost is classified as either direct or indirect materials. Direct materials requisitioned are recorded as Work-in-Process Inventory while indirect materials requisitioned are recorded as Manufacturing Overhead. Labor is also classified as direct or indirect. Direct labor is recorded as Work-in-Process Inventory, while indirect labor is recorded as Manufacturing Overhead.

Learning Objective 3:

Describe how companies analyze and record manufacturing overhead events during the conversion cycle.

Summary

Manufacturing overhead is a temporary account used to reflect the indirect manufacturing costs of the period. Actual manufacturing overhead costs, such as rent, supplies, and depreciation, are debited to the Manufacturing Overhead account. It is, therefore, necessary to assign or apply overhead costs to products. Most companies apply overhead to Work in Process throughout the period by using a predetermined overhead rate (estimated amount of overhead cost per cost driver). Work-in-Process Inventory will be debited and Manufacturing Overhead credited for an amount equal to the cost driver used times the predetermined overhead rate. Multiple overhead rates may be determined if activity-based costing is used. If underapplied or overapplied overhead results, the balance in manufacturing overhead must be closed.

Learning Objective 4:

Describe how companies analyze and record cost of goods manufactured and cost of goods sold during the conversion cycle.

Summary

As products are completed, the cost of goods manufactured is transferred from the Work-in-Process Inventory to Finished Goods Inventory. When the products are sold, the cost is then transferred from Finished Goods Inventory to Cost of Goods Sold.

Learning Objective 5:

Explain how companies communicate conversion cycle events to users.

Summary

The income statement reflects cost of goods sold during the period, and the balance sheet shows the ending balances in the related manufacturing inventory accounts. Internally, a cost of goods manufactured report is often prepared. It shows the costs for direct materials, direct labor and manufacturing overhead and shows the summary of the events during the period that affect the Raw Materials and Work-in-Process Inventory accounts.

Learning Objective 6: (Appendix)

Explain the differences among job order costing, process costing, and backflush costing.

Summary

A job-order costing system reports accumulated production costs based on individual jobs or batches. Is used by companies with jobs that are separate and distinct from one another. Process costing systems report accumulated production costs by departments because products are not individually identifiable. Industries that commonly use process costing systems produce homogeneous products in an assembly-line process. Backflush costing systems may be used by companies that have adopted the just-in-time philosophy. No separate inventory accounts are maintained for raw materials, work in process, or finished goods. It is assumed that raw materials purchased, labor used, and manufacturing overhead cost applied in the Cost of Goods Sold account will be expensed during the period.

Outline of Key Concepts

I. Introduction to manufacturing companies' inventory systems.

    A.   Cost accumulation in a manufacturing company is important for four reasons:

        1.   To determine the cost of products.

        2.   To determine if the selling prices for products were appropriate to achieve the company's goals.

        3.   To determine if the mix of products produced and sold was appropriate to achieve the company's goals, and

        4.   To determine the cost of goods sold for the period.

    B.   During the conversion cycle raw materials are converted into finished products using labor and other manufacturing resources.

    C.   The distinction between product and nonproduct cost is important.

        1.   Product cost--cost incurred in connection with the production of products for resale. Production costs are assets until the products are sold.

        2.   Nonproduct cost--cost incurred to sell the products or to administrate the business. Nonproduct costs may be assets or expenses, depending on whether they provide future benefits.

    D.   Manufacturing firms typically maintain three types of inventory accounts.

        1.   Raw materials inventory--reflects the costs for raw materials purchases.

        2.   Work-in-process inventory--reflects the costs of products started but not completed during the period.

        3.   Finished goods inventory--reflects the costs of all completed goods on hand, but not sold.

        4.   The cost flows through the inventory accounts are illustrated in Exhibit 10.2

II. Analyzing and recording events in the conversion cycle.

    A.   Analyzing and recording material events.

            1.   Acquisition cost of raw materials is recorded as Raw Materials Inventory.

            2.   When raw materials are requisitioned, the materials must be classified as either direct or indirect materials.

                    a.   Direct materials costs are transferred from Raw Material Inventory to Work-in-Process Inventory.

                    b.   Indirect materials costs are transferred from Raw Materials Inventory to Manufacturing Overhead.

    B.   Analyzing and recording labor events in the conversion cycle.

            1.   Cost of labor used must be classified as direct or indirect costs.

                    a.   Direct labor cost is recorded in the Work-in-Process Inventory account.

                    b.   Indirect labor cost is recorded in the Manufacturing Overhead account.

    C.   Analyzing and recording manufacturing overhead events in the conversion cycle.

            1.   Manufacturing overhead--a temporary account used to reflect the indirect manufacturing costs of the period. Includes the total of all indirect product costs.

            2.   The actual amounts of manufacturing overhead cost incurred during the period are recorded as debits to Manufacturing Overhead. Overhead costs must be assigned to the products themselves.

            3.   Applying manufacturing overhead--process of assigning overhead costs to the Work-in-Process Inventory.

                    a.   Predetermined overhead rate--estimated amount of overhead per cost driver. Is used to apply manufacturing overhead to production as the cost driver is used.

                    b.   Involves a debit to Work-in-Process Inventory and a credit to Manufacturing Overhead. Amount calculated by multiplying the predetermined overhead rate by the actual amount of the cost driver.

4. Overhead may be applied to production using multiple predetermined overhead rates determined from an activity-based costing (ABC) system. The steps in an ABC system include:

   a. Identify and classify production activities by level. Four levels are facility-sustaining level, product-sustaining level, batch-related level, or unit-related level.

   b. Determine the appropriate cost driver for each activity. See Exhibit 10.4.

   c. Estimate the amount of overhead related to each cost driver. There may be more than one cost pool for each activity level.

   d. Estimate the amounts of cost drivers to be used.

   e. Determine the predetermined overhead rate for each cost driver. The number of predetermined overhead rates depends on the number of cost pools used.

   f. Apply manufacturing overhead to Work-in-Process using the predetermined overhead rate.

5. Accounting for over- or underapplied manufacturing overhead.

   a. Underapplied overhead--debit balance in the manufacturing overhead account.

      i. The amount of overhead applied was not as much as the actual amount of manufacturing overhead cost incurred.

      ii. The cost of the products manufactured during the period is understated.

   b. Overapplied overhead--credit balance in the manufacturing overhead account.

      i. The amount of overhead applied to Work-in-Process was greater than the actual amount of overhead.

      ii. The cost of products manufactured during the period is overstated.

     c.   Balance must be closed.

         i.   Small balance--closed to Cost of Goods Sold.

         ii.   Large balance--closed to Cost of Goods Sold, Work-in-Process Inventory, and Finished Goods Inventory.

D.   Analyzing and recording cost of goods manufactured and cost of goods sold.

     1.   As products are completed, the cost of manufacturing the products (cost of goods manufactured) is transferred from Work-in-Process to Finished Goods Inventory.

     2.   When the products are sold, the cost of the finished goods is transferred to Cost of Goods Sold.

III. Communicating results of events in the conversion cycle.

A.   Cost of goods manufactured report--reports the costs for direct materials, direct labor, and manufacturing overhead and shows the summary of the events during the period that affected the Raw Materials and Work-in-Process Inventory accounts.

B.   Income statement reflects the cost of goods sold.

C.   Balance sheet--reports the manufacturing inventories in the current assets section.

D.   Notes to financial statements indicate the cost flow assumption (FIFO or LIFO).

IV. Appendix--Manufacturing Costing Systems.

A.   Job order costing systems--Used by companies with jobs that are separate and distinct from one another.

     1.   Accumulate production costs based on individual jobs or batches.

     2.   Accumulated production costs are recorded on a job cost sheet.

B.   Process costing systems-- Used by companies that manufacture homogeneous products in an assembly-line process.

     1.   Accumulate productions by departments because products are not individually identifiable.

2. Accumulated production costs are reflected in subsidiary work-in-process accounts for each department.

C. Backflush costing--assumes that the amount of raw materials purchased, direct labor used, and manufacturing overhead applied for the period will be expensed during the period. Recorded as Cost of Goods Sold.

1. Do not maintain separate inventory accounts for raw materials, work-in-process, and finished goods. Record the cost of any ending inventory in a current asset account called Raw and In-Process Inventory.

2. Traditional and backflush costing systems are compared in Exhibit 10.11.

Problem I

Indicate the correct answer by circling the appropriate letter.

1. Under an activity based costing system, testing the product will typically occur in the
_____ _____ activity level.
   a. facility sustaining
   b. product sustaining
   c. batch related
   d. unit related

2. Which of the following is not a primary reason that cost accumulation is important in a manufacturing business?
   a. to determine the cost of the product
   b. to determine if the selling prices for products were appropriate to achieve the company's goals
   c. to determine the cost of goods sold for the period
   d. all of the above are reasons that cost accumulation is important

3. Under an activity based costing system, ordering parts for use in production will typically occur in the _____ _____ activity level.
   a. facility sustaining
   b. product sustaining
   c. batch related
   d. unit related

4. All manufacturing firms have at least one activity in each of the four activity levels.
   a. true
   b. false

5. Under an activity based costing system, building maintenance costs will typically occur in the
_____ _____ activity level.
   a. facility sustaining
   b. product sustaining
   c. batch related
   d. unit related

6. Based on budgeted data, the assembly department should use 2,000 direct labor hours in the accounting period. Indirect labor costs are expected to be $100,000. Using direct labor hours as the cost driver, what amount will be added to work-in-process inventory if 300 direct labor hours are used in the first quarter of operations?
   a. $300
   b. $3,000
   c. $15,000
   d. $30,000

Use the following information for the next two questions:

The *Manufacturing Overhead - Machining* account had a credit balance of $29,000 at the end of the accounting period. Other account balances were as follows:

Work-in-process inventory	$ 100,000
Finished goods inventory	$ 300,000
Cost of goods sold	$1,600,000

7. If the overapplied manufacturing overhead is considered by management to be small, cost of goods sold will be _____.
   a. increased by $29,000
   b. decreased by $29,000
   c. increased by $23,200
   d. decreased by $23,200

8. If the overapplied manufacturing overhead is considered by management to be significant, cost of goods sold will be _____.
   a. increased by $29,000
   b. decreased by $29,000
   c. increased by $23,200
   d. decreased by $23,200

9. Under an activity based costing system, assembling the units produced will typically occur in the _____ _____ activity level.
   a. facility sustaining
   b. product sustaining
   c. batch related
   d. unit related

Problem II

Following is a list of important ideas and key concepts from the chapter. To test your knowledge of these terms, match the term with the definition by placing the number in the space provided.

_____ Actual manufacturing overhead   _____ Overapplied overhead
_____ Applied manufacturing overhead   _____ Predetermined overhead rate
_____ Cost of goods manufactured   _____ Product cost
_____ Cost pool   _____ Nonproduct cost
_____ Indirect product costs   _____ Underapplied overhead
_____ Manufacturing overhead

1. The excess of applied overhead over actual overhead for the accounting period

2. The amount of manufacturing overhead applied to Work-in-Process during the period, recorded as credits to Manufacturing Overhead for each cost pool based on the use of the cost driver

3. A group of costs that change in response to the same cost driver

4. A cost incurred to sell products or to administrate the business in a manufacturing company

5. The cost of manufactured products during the period, including direct materials, direct labor, and applied manufacturing overhead

6. The excess of actual overhead over applied overhead for the accounting period

7. The costs incurred to manufacture products that are not directly traced to the product, commonly called *manufacturing overhead*

8. A cost incurred in connection with the production of products for resale in a manufacturing company

9. The amount of manufacturing overhead incurred during the period, recorded as debits to Manufacturing Overhead for each cost pool when the cost is incurred

10. The collection of temporary accounts used to record the indirect product manufacturing costs of the period

11. The estimated amount of overhead per cost driver; it is used to apply overhead to production throughout the period as the cost driver is used

Problem III

Complete the following sentences by filling in the correct response.

1. Activities that maintain the productive capacity of the company will occur in the
   _____ _____ level in an activity based costing system.

2. In the conversion cycle, _____ _____ are converted into finished
   products using _____ and _____ resources.

3. A _____ cost is incurred in connection with production of products for resale while a
   _____ cost is incurred to sell the products or to administer business.

4. A manufacturing firm typically maintains _____ _____,
   _____ and _____ _____ inventories.

5. In an activity based costing system, a cost driver, such as number of machine hours used, will
   typically occur in the _____ _____ level.

6. Costs cannot be combined into a _____ _____ unless they are represented by
   the same _____ _____.

7. Underapplied overhead occurs when _____ overhead costs exceed the _____
   overhead costs.

Problem IV

In the space provided, indicate whether the cost will be considered a product (P) or a nonproduct
(NP) cost.

_____1. Freight-in on raw materials purchased
_____2. Cost of placing an advertisement in a local newspaper
_____3. Indirect labor
_____4. Depreciation on the manufacturing plant
_____5. Shipping costs on merchandise sold
_____6. Receptionist salary (for the President)
_____7. Direct materials
_____8. Salaries of plant workers
_____9. Utilities in the administrative headquarters
_____10. Indirect materials

Problem V

D Company manufactures a specialty mulching product from certain pulp woods. Selected transactions for D company are presented below:

a. Purchased $50,000 of raw materials with terms 2/10, n/30 (use the net price method).

b. Raw materials costing $18,000 are transferred into the production process. Of this amount, $16,000 is considered direct materials and $2,000 is considered indirect materials.

c. Employee's salaries (ignore withholding) paid were $5,000 for direct labor (400 hours), $1,000 for indirect labor, and $3,000 for selling and administrative.

d. Depreciation for the month was $12,000 on production equipment and $3,500 on office equipment.

e. Expired insurance costs (prepaid in the previous period) on coverage related to production facilities and office facilities were $2,000 and $1,000, respectively.

f. D Company maintains only one cost pool and applies its overhead based on $10 per direct labor hour.

Required: Prepare the entries in general journal form to record the preceding events.

General Journal

Date	Account Title	Debit	Credit

Problem V (continued)

General Journal			
Date	*Account Title*	*Debit*	*Credit*

Pause and Reflect:

Some companies have highly-automated manufacturing facilities. Therefore, they incur little direct labor costs. Thus, these companies often do not record direct labor costs as a separate item. How might these automated companies record their direct labor costs?

Solutions for Chapter 10

Problem 1

1. b
2. d
3. c
4. b
5. a
6. c
7. b
8. d
9. d

Problem II

9 Actual manufacturing overhead
2 Applied manufacturing overhead
5 Cost of goods manufactured
3 Cost pool
7 Indirect product costs
10 Manufacturing overhead

1 Overapplied overhead
11 Predetermined overhead rate
8 Product cost
4 Nonproduct cost
6 Underapplied overhead

Problem III

1. facility-sustaining
2. raw materials, labor, manufacturing
3. product, nonproduct
4. raw materials, work-in-process, finished goods
5. unit related
6. cost pool, cost driver
7. actual, applied

Problem IV

1. P
2. NP
3. P
4. P
5. NP

6. NP
7. P
8. P
9. NP
10. P

Problem V

General Journal

Date	Account Title	Debit	Credit
a)	Raw materials inventory	49,000	
	Accounts payable		49,000
b)	Work-in-process inventory	16,000	
	Manufacturing overhead	2,000	
	Raw materials inventory		18,000
c)	Work-in-process inventory	5,000	
	Manufacturing overhead	1,000	
	Salaries expense	3,000	
	Cash		9,000
d)	Manufacturing overhead	12,000	
	Depreciation expense	3,500	
	Accumulated Depreciation		15,500
e)	Manufacturing overhead	2,000	
	Insurance expense	1,000	
	Prepaid insurance		3,000
f)	Work-in-process	4,000	
	Manufacturing overhead		4,000

Pause and Reflect:

In highly-automated manufacturing facilities, direct labor costs may comprise only 5 to 10 percent of total production costs. In such cases, it may not be cost beneficial to collect direct labor costs separately and charge them to work in process. Instead, both direct and indirect labor costs are recorded in the manufacturing overhead account. No attempt is made to trace direct labor costs to jobs or departments.

Chapter 11 Cash: Management and Control

Learning Objective 1:

Explain how companies manage cash by investing excess cash on a short-term basis and raising additional cash through short-term borrowing.

Summary

Companies invest idle cash to earn interest and increase net income in order to remain in a position to pay current liabilities as they become due. Excess cash may be invested in temporary investments such as treasury bills, certificates of deposit, or money market accounts. When a company has a temporary cash shortage, it must obtain funds from outside sources. Some of these sources include financial institution loans, suppliers who issue notes payable, companies that issue commercial paper, companies that factor accounts receivable, and companies that discount notes receivable. Interest is the cost of borrowing these funds.

Learning Objective 2:

Identify the process of and reasons for factoring accounts receivable and discounting notes receivable.

Summary

Factoring accounts receivables involves businesses that sell some or all of their accounts receivable in order to raise cash. The company selling the receivables receives cash from the factor (buyer), less a fee (which can be very high) that the factor charges for its services. Discounting notes receivables involves selling notes receivables to banks or other third parties who provide the business with immediate cash. The discount rate is the interest the purchaser of the note wants to earn. Notes receivables may be discounted with or without recourse.

Learning Objective 3:

Describe cash-related internal controls businesses use.

Summary

Controls on cash receipts include: physically safeguarding the cash, separating duties of those with custody of cash from those who keep the accounting records, assigning duties so that cash is deposited and recorded as soon as possible after receipt, and having independent checks on cash balances and cash handling procedures. Control procedures over cash disbursements include separating the responsibilities of check writing, check signing, check mailing, and keeping the accounting records; and ensuring that payments are properly authorized. The cash balance should be verified by completing a bank reconciliation.

Outline of Key Concepts

I. Cash management involves a trade-off between not having enough cash to make necessary transactions and having cash on hand that generates little or no return.

    A. Companies hold cash for a number of reasons.

        1. To pay vendors and employees.

        2. As a precaution against unforeseen events.

        3. To take advantage of unforeseen short-term profit-making opportunities.

        4. The timing of cash receipts and cash outflows is crucial to the survival of any organization.

    B. Idle or excess cash should be invested so a company can earn interest and increase its net income in order to remain in a position to pay its current liabilities.

        1. Temporary investments--short-term investments in liquid assets for a period of less than one year.

            a. Treasury bills--short-term loans to the U.S. government. Are virtually risk free and typically pay a low rate of interest.

            b. Certificates of deposit--guaranteed savings deposits placed in banks or savings and loan institutions which are insured by the FDIC or FSLIC. Deposits can be withdrawn at any time, but there is a substantial penalty for early withdrawal.

            c. Money market accounts--similar to checking accounts except that the banks where they are held pay interest on the amount of funds deposited and require that investors maintain a minimum balance in the accounts. Interest rates are usually lower than CD or Treasury rates.

    C. When there is a shortage of cash, a company must obtain funds from outside sources.

        1. Short-term loans from financial institutions.

            a. Note payable--short-term promise to pay cash supported by a written promissory note.

b.   Line of credit--preapproved loan up to a maximum prespecified amount. A company can then borrow the amount of cash it needs at any time, up to the amount of the credit limit and any other written terms.

2.   Notes payable from suppliers--may be required at the time of purchase or at a later date to settle the borrower's account payable due to the supplier.

   a.   Interest-bearing note--debt instrument with an explicitly stated interest rate.

   b.   Noninterest-bearing note--does not have an interest rate specified on the face of the note. Supplier gives the business less money or goods/services than the amount shown on the note's face value.

3.   Issuing commercial paper--short-term note payable issued in large amounts by big companies with very good credit ratings.

   a.   Maturity is usually 270 days or less, and interest rates are slightly below the prime rate.

4.   Factoring accounts receivable--businesses sell some or all of their accounts receivable in order to raise cash.

   a.   Factor--buyer of accounts receivables. Usually assumes responsibility for collecting the receivables purchased.

   b.   The seller receives immediate cash from the factor, less a fee (which can be very high) that the factor charges for its services.

5.   Discounting Notes Receivable--businesses sell notes receivable to banks and other third parties who provide the businesses with immediate cash.

   a.   Discount--difference between the maturity value of the note and the cash proceeds received by the business.

      i.   Discount = Maturity x Discount x Discount
            amount   value   rate   period

   b.   Note may be transferred with or without recourse.

II. Internal controls are important for protecting cash.

    A.   Procedures to protect cash receipts include:

        1.   Physically safeguarding the cash.

            a.   Use of cash register and sales slip given to customer.

        2.   Separating duties of those with custody of cash from those who keep the accounting records.

            a.   Remittance advice--part of customer invoice returned with the customer's payment.

            b.   Lockbox collection system--a business establishes bank accounts at various locations around the area where their customers live. Customers mail their payments to the post office of the business's bank nearest to them. The bank collects the cash receipts, deposits the cash into the business's account, and forwards a list of the customer receipts to the business.

        3.   Assigning duties so that cash is deposited and recorded as soon as possible after receipt.

        4.   Having independent checks on cash balances and cash handling procedures.

    B.   Controls over cash disbursements include:

        1.   Separating the responsibilities of check writing, check signing, check mailing, and keeping the accounting records.

        2.   Ensuring that payments are properly authorized.

    C.   Verifying the cash balance with a bank reconciliation.

        1.   Bank statements show all the transactions in each customer's cash account for the month, including:

            a.   Beginning and ending balance of the account according to the bank's books.

            b.   Deposits made to the account during the period.

            c.   Amounts withdrawn from the account during the period.

d.   Any additional charges or credits to the account according to the bank, such as service charges or interest earned.

2.   Business may be aware of some transactions affecting cash that are unknown by the bank.

   a.   Outstanding checks--written and mailed by the business and deducted in the business's cash account, but not yet processed by the bank.

   b.   Deposits in transit--deposits the business has recorded in its cash account and has sent to the bank or put in the night depository, but the bank has not received and recorded.

3.   Bank reconciliation--process that requires that the company periodically adjust the recorded cash amounts in its records to reflect any differences between its cash balance and the cash balance according to the bank.

   a.   Should be performed by an employee who is involved in neither the receipt nor the deposit of cash, nor the approval or payment of cash disbursements.

   b.   Highlights any differences due to timing of withdrawals, deposits, and other account increases and decreases. Allows unrecorded items to be reflected in the records of the business and the bank and for errors to be corrected.

   c.   Two-column approach reconciles the cash balance according to the bank and the cash balance according to the books to an adjusted "correct" balance.

D.   Controlling "small" cash disbursements.

1.   Imprest cash accounts--established for fixed amount and commonly used either to pay small amounts or to handle payroll payments.

   a.   Petty cash fund--an imprest account maintained for the immediate use of small amounts of cash. Total of receipts plus the remaining cash should equal the authorized amount in the petty cash fund.

   b.   Payroll account--Only one authorization required to approve disbursements of all paychecks.

Problem I

Indicate whether the following statements are either true (T) or false (F).

_____1.   Cash on hand generally generates little or no return.
_____2.   Treasury Bills are guaranteed by the U.S. government.
_____3.   Interest rates paid on certificates of deposits will generally be at the prime rate of interest.
_____4.   Factoring accounts receivable allows a company to immediately receive cash rather than waiting for payment from customers.
_____5.   A note payable is a short-term promise to pay cash and is supported by a written promissory note.
_____6.   A disadvantage of a line of credit is that the company typically is charged interest at a higher rate than might otherwise be available.
_____7.   The risk of default on commercial paper is high since it is usually issued by small companies in uncertain financial condition.
_____8.   Commercial paper is often purchased by pension funds and large institutional investors.
_____9.   The bank reconciliation should be performed by the person responsible for depositing the cash in the bank.
_____10.   An adjusting entry will be made to the cash account in the general ledger to account for any outstanding checks on the bank reconciliation.
_____11.   Routine transactions involving relatively small amounts of cash should not need authorization by upper-level management.
_____12.   A lock-box system improves a company's internal control procedures.

Problem II

Indicate the correct answer by circling the appropriate letter.

1. Which of the following is not an advantage of investing idle cash in Treasury Bills?

    a. the investment is virtually risk free
    b. the investment is easily converted back to cash
    c. the investment pays a high rate of return
    c. neither (a) nor (b) is an advantage of Treasury Bills

2. Short Inc. signed a 90-day, noninterest-bearing note with a face value of $207,000 with one of its suppliers. At the time the note was signed, Short Inc. received $200,000 in merchandise. What is the annual rate of interest charged on the note?
    a. 13.7%
    b. 10.2%
    c. 14.2%
    d. 9.4%

Use the following information for the next two questions:

On February 1, 19X7, Freeland Company discounted a $20,000 note receivable at the bank at a discount rate of 12%. The note had been received 30 days earlier and had a 120-day maturity bearing an interest rate of 10%.

3. How much will Freeland receive from the bank on February 1?
    a. $20,000
    b. $20,046
    c. $20,191
    d. $19,345

4. How much will the bank receive from Freeland's customer on the maturity date of the note?
    a. $20,000
    b. $19,456
    c. $20,789
    d. $20,658

Problem III

The following is a list of important ideas and key concepts from the chapter. To test your knowledge of these terms, match the term with the definition by placing the number in the space provided.

_____ Bank reconciliation	_____ Maker of note
_____ Bank statements	_____ Nonsufficient funds checks (NSF)
_____ Certificates of deposit	_____ Outstanding checks
_____ Commercial paper	_____ Payee of a note
_____ Deposits in transit	_____ Petty cash fund
_____ Discounted notes receivable	_____ Prime rate
_____ Factor	_____ Remittance advice
_____ Factoring accounts receivable	_____ Service charge
_____ Imprest Cash accounts	_____ Temporary investments
_____ Line of credit	_____ With recourse
_____ Lockbox collection system	_____ Without recourse

1. A document returned (remitted) by customers with payment to ensure proper credit to their account

2. Notes receivable from a customer that a business can sell to a bank or other third party

3. No further obligation by the party (company) transferring a note or accounts receivable balance if the issuing party fails to pay

4. A control procedure to highlight and allow adjustments for any differences between a business's cash balance and the bank's recorded cash balance due to withdrawals, deposits, and other account transactions

5. A system to collect cash due from customers who mail payments to a post office near a business's bank. The bank collects the cash receipts, deposits the cash, and sends the business a listing of the customer receipts

6. Fees charged by banks for benefits provided to customers

7. Cash deposited in the bank and recorded on the company's books but not yet recorded by the bank

8. The interest rate banks charge to their best customers

9. An imprest account, or fund, maintained for the immediate use of small amounts of cash

10. Selling some or all of accounts receivable to a third party for a fee in order to obtain immediate cash

11. The party borrowing money using a promissory note

12. Cash accounts commonly set up to pay small, routine cash amounts or payroll

13. An obligation to pay by the party (company) transferring a note or accounts receivable balance if the issuing party fails to do so

14. Reports sent regularly (usually monthly) by banks to their customers showing all transactions in the customer's cash account during the period

15. Short-term investments of cash in other liquid assets

16. Guaranteed savings deposits placed in banks or savings and loans for periods of three months to five years

17. Checks written, mailed, and deducted from a business's Cash account, but not processed by the bank

18. A preapproved loan that allows the borrower to request money when needed up to the total preapproved amount of the line

19. Checks written for amounts that are greater than the balance of the bank accounts on which they are written

20. A third party that buys some or all of a business's accounts receivable for cash

21. The party lending money using a promissory note

22. Short-term notes payable in large amounts issued typically by large companies with very good credit ratings

Problem IV

The following information related to the Cash account is available for the month of December:

a. The bank statement balance at December 31 is $23,967

b. The following checks were written by the company in December but have not cleared the bank:

Check Number	Amount
11,234	$1,789
12,435	$2,678
12,450	$1,500

c. The following debit memos from the bank were included in the December bank statement:

Nonsufficient Funds Check $550
Service charge $150

d. The company incorrectly recorded a deposit from a customer as $960 instead of $690.

e. There was a $4,500 deposit in transit.

f. The ending balance per books was $23,470.

Required: Prepare a bank reconciliation for the month of December.

Bank Reconciliation
December 31

Pause and Reflect:

Some companies sell their accounts receivable despite the potentially high fees charged by the factor. Why would companies continue to sell their accounts receivable under these terms?

_____
_____
_____
_____
_____
_____
_____
_____
_____
_____
_____
_____
_____
_____
_____
_____
_____
_____
_____
_____
_____
_____
_____
_____

Solutions for Chapter 11

Problem 1

1. T	7. F
2. T	8. T
3. F	9. F
4. T	10. F
5. T	11. T
6. T	12. T

Problem II

1. c
2. c
3. b
4. d

Problem III

4	Bank reconciliation	11	Maker of note
14	Bank statements	19	Nonsufficient funds checks (NSF)
16	Certificates of deposit	17	Outstanding checks
22	Commercial paper	21	Payee of a note
7	Deposits in transit	9	Petty cash fund
2	Discounted notes receivable	8	Prime rate
20	Factor	1	Remittance advice
10	Factoring accounts receivable	6	Service charge
12	Imprest Cash accounts	15	Temporary investments
18	Line of credit	13	With recourse
5	Lockbox collection system	3	Without recourse

Problem IV

Bank Reconciliation
December 31

Balance per bank		$23,967
Add: Deposits in transit	4,500	
Deduct: Outstanding checks	<5,967>	
Adjusted balance per books		$22,500
Balance per books		$23,470
Deduct:		
NSF check	550	
Service charge	150	
Correction of error	270	
Adjusted balance per books		$22,500

Pause and Reflect:

One possible explanation is a severe cash flow problem. A company may be unable to generate enough cash sales plus customer account collections to meet current obligations to suppliers and employees. Companies with seasonal sales may find this to be particularly true. In addition, because of cash flow difficulties, a company may not be viewed as a good credit risk for short-term borrowing from a financial institution. Chronic cash flow problems may be a symptom of poor sales or poor collection practices. Therefore, selling accounts receivable may be the quickest and easiest way to generate cash inflows.

Another possible explanation is cost versus benefit. It may be less costly to turn collection of receivables over to a third party. Although the factor's fee usually includes a reserve for uncollectible accounts, the company would not have to maintain a large credit/collections department. Therefore, the cost of factoring accounts receivable may be less than maintaining a collections department.

Chapter 12 Revenue and Expenditure Cycles: Analysis and Control

Learning Objective 1:

Discuss ways in which managers can evaluate operating activities.

Summary

An effective way to evaluate specific aspects of a company's operations is to analyze the data contained in its financial statements. Analysis of a company's financial statements highlights differences between planned and actual performance. Management analyzes the differences to determine the causes of the differences, what may have gone wrong, and who may have been responsible. There are three general approaches to financial statement analysis: (1) horizontal analysis, (2) vertical analysis, and (3) ratio analysis.

Learning Objective 2:

Identify what type of information results from vertical and horizontal analyses.

Summary

Horizontal analysis is a type of financial statement analysis that compares one item to itself over time on both a dollar amount and percentage basis to indicate the amount of change that occurred over time. It is helpful for discovering trends in financial statement relationships or for focusing on changes in underlying operating activities or the business environment. Vertical analysis shows the relationship of all the other items to some base item, or a reference point, within that particular statement. It indicates the relative importance of various items on the financial statements.

Learning Objective 3:

Identify the type of information obtained from ratio analyses and what it tells the user of accounting information.

Summary

Ratio analysis focuses specifically on interrelationships of accounts to answer questions like: Is inventory at the level we expect given the amount of cost of goods sold for the period? The potential explanations for results of ratio analysis are usually limited to the types of transactions underlying the relationship.

Outline of Key Concepts

I. Companies use financial statements to analyze operations.

    A. Managers must determine and assess whether the business is better or worse off than in previous periods.

        1. Analyze the company's performance by using industry reports.

        2. Analyze the data contained in the company's financial statements.

            a. Highlight differences between actual and planned performance.

            b. Management is responsible for determining the cause of the differences noted; what was better than expected; what may have gone wrong; who may have been responsible; and how to address and fix the problems and plan better for the future.

            c. Must have a standard of comparison--past relationships, planned objectives, or external sources, such as Dun & Bradstreet.

    B. Analysis shows managers where to focus their efforts.

II. There are three major approaches to financial statement analysis to assess a company's short-term liquidity, results of operations, and long-term profitability.

    A. Horizontal analysis--system of financial statement analysis that shows a comparison of each item on a financial statement with that same item on statements from previous periods.

        1. On both a dollar amount and percentage basis to indicate the amount of change that occurred over time.

        2. Helpful for discovering trends in financial statement relationships in order to predict short-term results for financial statement items.

        3. By focusing on changes in financial statement items, changes in underlying operating activities or changes in the business environment may be revealed.

    B. Vertical analysis--system of financial statement analysis that shows the size of selected items in one financial statement relative to some base item for the same period.

        1. Indicates the relative importance of various items on the financial statements.

2. Rely on percentages of change. Percentages avoid distortion caused by comparing businesses of different sizes.

3. Vertical analysis of income statements uses sales as the base item; the balance sheet uses total assets.

4. Vertical analysis used with horizontal analysis reveals trends in financial data relationships.

C. Ratio analysis--involves creating ratios that use two or more accounts related by the transactions they represent. Ratio analysis focuses specifically on interrelationships of accounts.

1. When ratios reflect both income statement and balance sheet items, averages for the balance sheet items must be used.

2. Exhibit 12.8 lists commonly used financial ratios.

3. Ratios used to evaluate purchasing and inventory management decisions.

   a. Inventory turnover--indicates how many times during the period the company completed the sequence of events from acquiring inventory through the sale of inventory.

   b. Average selling period ratio--represents the number of days it takes to sell the average amount of inventory.

4. Ratios used to evaluate disbursement decisions.

   a. Payables turnover--ratio of cash expenses, or expenses that require a cash payment, to the average current liabilities, excluding the principal portions of bank loans.

   b. Payment period ratio--measures the average number of days required to pay the average amount of current operating liabilities.

5. Ratios used to evaluate credit decisions.

   a. Accounts receivable turnover--indicates whether the amount of accounts receivable is appropriate for the company's sales level.

   b. Average collection period ratio--measures the average number of days it takes to collect the average balance in accounts receivable.

6. Ratios used to evaluate pricing decisions.

    a. Gross margin ratio--measures, in percentage terms, that portion of sales revenue available after deducting the cost of goods sold.

    b. Return on sales ratio--measures that portion of sales revenue remaining after deducting all operating expenses. Is an indication of the business's overall profitability.

7. Ratios used to evaluate solvency (a business's ability to pay its short-term financial obligations). Solvency ratios measure the viability of the business in the short term.

    a. Current ratio--determined by comparing total current assets with total current liabilities. Measures the adequacy of a company's current assets to meet its current obligations.

    b. Quick ratio or acid-test ratio--ratio of liquid assets to current liabilities. Quick assets are cash and cash equivalents, temporary investments, and accounts receivables.

Problem I

Indicate whether the following statements are either true (T) or false (F).

_____1. Horizontal analysis is a system of financial statement analysis that shows the size of selected items in one financial statement relative to some basic item for one period.

_____2. Vertical analysis avoids certain distortions caused by comparing businesses of different sizes.

_____3. Ratio analysis may use interrelated accounts from two different financial statements.

_____4. The current ratio is a more conservative test of solvency than is the quick ratio.

_____5. Managers must balance the costs of ordering inventory at frequent intervals with the cost of carrying too much inventory.

_____6. Credit sales rather than total sales should be used in the accounts receivable turnover ratio.

_____7. The operating cycle is the sum of the selling period and the collection period.

_____8. The last phase of the management cycle is the evaluation phase.

Problem II

Indicate the correct answer by circling the appropriate letter.

1. Which of the following would not be used to evaluate expenditure cycle decisions?
   a. inventory turnover ratio
   b. payable turnover ratio
   c. payment period ratio
   d. current ratio

Use the following information for the next two questions:

Z Company had $200,000 in total current assets and $140,000 in total current liabilities as of the end of the year. Total current assets consisted of the following:

Cash	$15,000
Temporary investments	$25,000
Accounts receivable	$85,000
Inventory	$75,000

2. Z Company's current ratio is _____.
   a. 1.43
   b. 7.00
   c. .95
   d. 2.34

3. Z Company's quick ratio is _____.
   a. 1.43
   b. .95
   c. 2.04
   d. .89

4. Which of the following would not be used to evaluate revenue cycle decisions?
   a. accounts receivable turnover ratio
   b. quick ratio
   c. average collection period ratio
   d. gross margin ratio

5. Y Company has an accounts receivable turnover ratio of 7.2 and a 6.1 inventory turnover ratio. What is Y Company's operating cycle?
   a. 13.3 days
   b. 110.5 days
   c. 87.4 days
   d. 93.7 days

6. Which of the following is used to evaluate a company's solvency?
   a. current ratio
   b. return on sales ratio
   c. inventory turnover ratio
   d. all of the above are used to evaluate solvency

7. X Company has an accounts receivable turnover ratio of 30.8 and an inventory turnover ratio of 16.2. What is X Company's average collection period?
   a. 47 days
   b. 11.85 days
   c. 22.5 days
   d. 15.7 days

Problem III

Following is a list of important ideas and key concepts from the chapter. To test your knowledge of these terms, match the term with the definition by placing the number in the space provided.

_____ Cash equivalents .... _____ Operating cycle
_____ Horizontal analysis .... _____ Solvency
_____ Ratio analysis .... _____ Vertical analysis

1. A business's ability to pay its short-term financial obligations.

2. The cycle beginning with sales converting inventory into accounts receivable; and subsequent collection of accounts receivable, which the company then uses to pay off its liabilities

3. Analysis of the relative size of items to a base item within one statement for one period

4. Assets that are one step removed from cash; for example, the next step in their normal cycle is conversion to cash

5. Comparison of each item on a financial statement with that same item on statements from previous periods

6. The relationship between accounts or groups of accounts from the same statement or related items on two different statements expressed as one number divided by another number

Problem IV

Complete the following sentences by filling in the correct response.

_____1. The average collection period is calculated by dividing the number of days in the year by the _____ _____ _____ ratio.

_____2. The _____ ratio is also known as the acid-test ratio and is considered a strict measure of the company's ability to meet _____ _____.

_____3. The current ratio is determined by dividing total _____ _____ by total _____ _____ and it measures the ability of the company to meet its current obligations.

_____4. The inventory turnover ratio is calculated by dividing _____ ____ _____ _____ by the average balance in the _____ account.

_____5. When performing a vertical analysis of financial statements, income statement items will be divided by _____ _____ and balance sheet items will be divided by _____ _____.

Problem V

The financial statements of the Sugar Company are presented below:

Sugar Company
Income Statement
Current Year

Revenues:		
Net sales		$600,000
Costs and Expenses:		
Cost of goods sold	250,000	
Selling and administrative expenses	120,000	
Interest expense	35,000	
Income tax expense	85,000	490,000
Net income		$110,000

Sugar Company
Balance Sheet
December 31 of

	Current year	Previous year
Current assets:		
Cash	$ 49,000	$ 46,000
Accounts receivable, net	133,000	167,000
Inventory	47,000	53,000
Prepaid expenses	4,000	5,000
Total current assets	$233,000	$271,000
Property, plant and equipment:		
Land and buildings	335,000	285,000
Less: accumulated depreciation	< 95,000>	< 55,000>
Total property, plant and equipment	$240,000	$230,000
Total assets	$473,000	$501,000
Current liabilities:		
Accounts payable	$ 95,000	$114,000
Accrued expenses	45,000	41,000
Total current liabilities	$140,000	$155,000
Long-term liabilities:		
Notes payable	$200,000	$240,000
Total Stockholders' equity	$133,000	$106,000
Total liabilities and stockholders' equity	$473,000	$501,000

Problem V (continued)

a. Compute the following ratios for the current year using the financial statements provided on the previous page:

    1. Current ratio

    2. Inventory turnover ratio

    3. Accounts receivable turnover ratio (all sales are on credit)

    4. Gross margin ratio

b. Prepare a horizontal analysis of the balance sheet.

Sugar Company
Horizontal Analysis as of December 31

	Current Year	Previous Year	Difference Amount	Percent
Current assets:				
Cash	$ 49,000	$ 46,000		
Accounts receivable, net	133,000	167,000		
Inventory	47,000	53,000		
Prepaid expenses	4,000	5,000		
Total current assets	$233,000	$271,000		
Property, plant and equipment:				
Land and buildings	335,000	285,000		
Less: accumulated depreciation	< 95,000>	< 55,000>		
Total property, plant and equipment	$240,000	$230,000		
Total assets	$473,000	$501,000		
Current liabilities:				
Accounts payable	$ 95,000	$114,000		
Accrued expenses	45,000	41,000		
Total current liabilities	$140,000	$155,000		
Long-term liabilities:				
Notes payable	$200,000	$240,000		
Total Stockholders' equity	$133,000	$106,000		
Total liabilities and stockholders' equity	$473,000	$501,000		

    Introduction to Accounting: An Integrated Approach, 1st Edition

Pause and Reflect:

Explain how it would be possible for a company to have an acceptable current ratio but still be unable to pay its current obligations.

_____
_____
_____
_____
_____
_____
_____
_____
_____
_____
_____
_____
_____
_____
_____
_____
_____
_____
_____
_____
_____
_____
_____

Solutions for Chapter 12

Problem 1

1. F	5. T
2. T	6. T
3. T	7. T
4. F	8. T

Problem II

1. d
2. a
3. d
4. b
5. b
6. a
7. b

Problem III

4	Cash equivalents	2	Operating cycle
5	Horizontal analysis	1	Solvency
6	Ratio analysis	3	Vertical analysis

Problem IV

1. accounts receivable turnover
2. quick, current obligations
3. current assets, current liabilities
4. cost of goods sold, inventory
5. total sales, total assets

Problem V

a.1. Current ratio = $\dfrac{\text{Total current assets}}{\text{Total current liabilities}}$ $\dfrac{\$233,000}{\$140,000}$ = 1.66

2. $\dfrac{\text{Inventory}}{\text{turnover ratio}}$ = $\dfrac{\text{Cost of goods sold}}{\text{Average Inventory}}$ $\dfrac{\$250,000}{(\$47,000 + \$53,000)/2}$ = 5

3. $\dfrac{\text{Accounts receivable}}{\text{turnover ratio}}$ = $\dfrac{\text{Net credit sales}}{\text{Average accounts receivable}}$

   $\dfrac{\$600,000}{(\$133,000 + \$167,000)/2}$ = 4

4. Gross margin ratio = $\dfrac{\text{Gross profit}}{\text{Net sales}}$ $\dfrac{\$350,000}{\$600,000}$ = 58.3%

b.

Sugar Company
Horizontal Analysis as of December 31

	Current year	Previous year	Difference Amount	Percent
Current assets:				
Cash	$ 49,000	$ 46,000	$ 3,000	6.5%
Accounts receivable, net	133,000	167,000	<34,000>	<20.4%>
Inventory	47,000	53,000	< 6,000>	<11.3%>
Prepaid expenses	4,000	5,000	< 1,000>	<20.0%>
Total current assets	$233,000	$271,000	<38,000>	<14.0%>
Property, plant and equipment:				
Land and buildings	335,000	285,000	50,000	17.5%
Less: accumulated depreciation	< 95,000>	< 55,000>	40,000	72.7%
Total property, plant and equip.	$240,000	$230,000	10,000	4.4%
Total assets	$473,000	$501,000	<28,000>	< 5.6%>
Current liabilities:				
Accounts payable	$ 95,000	$114,000	<19,000>	<16.7%>
Accrued expenses	45,000	41,000	4,000	9.8%
Total current liabilities	$140,000	$155,000	<15,000>	< 9.7%>
Long-term liabilities:				
Notes payable	$200,000	$240,000	<40,000>	<16.7%>
Total Stockholders' equity	$133,000	$106,000	17,000	16.0%
Total liabilities and stockholders' equity	$473,000	$501,000	<28,000>	< 5.6%>

Pause and Reflect:

The current ratio is calculated by dividing current assets by current liabilities. Current assets include cash and cash equivalents, accounts receivable, notes receivable, inventories, and miscellaneous other prepaid assets. A current ratio may be acceptable, but if inventories or accounts receivables make up a large portion of the current assets, there may not be sufficient cash to pay current obligations. If the inventory level is high, this may mean sales are weak. If sales are not being made, then cash will not flow into the company. High levels of accounts receivable could indicate poor collection practices. If accounts are not being collected in a timely manner, then insufficient cash inflows may occur. In either case, current obligations might not be met.

Chapter 13   Conversion Cycle: Analysis and Control

Learning Objective 1:

Describe how to use variances to evaluate the efficiency of the conversion cycle.

Summary

Efficiency relates to whether a company's goals were achieved using the best combination of the company's resources. Efficiency is measured by comparing the actual inputs to the expected inputs. Variances are the differences between budgeted and actual financial amounts of inputs. A flexible budget is prepared to reflect the actual production level, so that actual costs can be compared to planned costs at the same level of activity.

Learning Objective 2:

Explain how to use variances to evaluate the use of direct materials and direct labor.

Summary

The direct labor price variance indicates whether the wage rate incurred per hour of direct labor was greater or less than expected. The direct labor usage variance indicates whether workers are producing products in the amount of time allowed. The direct materials price variance shows whether the price incurred per unit of direct materials input was greater or less than the price expected. The direct materials usage variance shows whether the actual quantity of direct materials used during the period was greater or less than the amount budgeted. In a JIT environment a direct materials inventory variance is calculated. It indicates whether more or less material was purchased than used.

Learning Objective 3:

Explain how managers use variances to evaluate overhead.

Summary

Actual overhead may differ from planned amounts for two reasons: (1) the overhead costs are more (or less) than expected or (2) production used more (or less) of the cost driver than expected. An overhead price variance is the difference between the actual amount of overhead incurred for the period and the amount of overhead applied to production during the period. The price variance is calculated for each individual overhead cost pool. The overhead usage variance is the difference between the overhead applied to production during the period and the flexible budget amount of overhead for the period. It shows whether the amount of overhead applied was greater (or less) than the amount budgeted.

Learning Objective 4:

Describe how companies determine which variances require additional investigation.

Summary

Most companies use a management-by-exception approach to investigating variances. Criteria must be established to determine which variances will be investigated. The absolute size of the variance is one consideration. A second consideration is the presence of trends in variances. Management must also consider the costs of investigating variances.

Learning Objective 5:

Explain how companies use other performance measures to evaluate quality and processes.

Summary

One way companies measure quality is by calculating and analyzing quality costs. There are four types of quality costs: (1) prevention cost, (2) appraisal cost, (3) internal failure cost, and (4) external failure cost. Processes may be measured by determining on-time deliveries, calculating delivery time, determining throughput time, and measuring nonvalue-added activities.

Outline of Key Concepts

I. An introduction to effectiveness and efficiency measures.

    A. Effectiveness--relates to whether the goals of the company were achieved during the period.

        1. Measured by comparing the actual outputs of the company to the expected outputs.

    B. Efficiency--relates to whether the goals were achieved using the best combination of the company's resources.

        1. Measured by comparing the actual inputs of the company to the expected inputs.

        2. Variances--differences between budgeted and actual financial amounts of inputs.

            a. Management-by-exception--investigate only the variances that are significant.

            b. Standard cost--predetermined cost estimate of a particular operating input.

                i. Standard quantity--estimated amount of the input.

                ii. Standard price--estimated cost of the input.

    C. First step in the analysis and control of the conversion cycle is to compare the budgeted costs of production inputs to the actual costs incurred.

        1. Master budget set for a certain level of production is inappropriate to use if the actual production level was different from the planned level.

        2. Flexible budget--reflects the actual production level of the period.

            a. Actual costs incurred can be compared to planned costs at the same level of production.

            b. Computation of flexible budget cost requires multiplying the standard cost of an input times the actual output quantity.

    D. Direct labor variance analysis examines the difference between the actual and flexible budget results for direct labor.

1. Direct labor price variance--indicates whether the wage rate incurred per hour of direct labor was greater or less than expected.

    a. Assumed to be controllable by the human resources and/or the production department.

    b. Calculated as: (Actual price x Actual quantity of hours worked) - (Standard price x Actual quantity of hours worked).

        i. If the actual price is greater than the standard price, the variance is unfavorable.

        ii. If the actual price is less than the standard price, the variance is favorable.

2. Direct labor usage variance--indicates whether workers are producing products in the amount of time allowed.

    a. Controllable by the production department.

    b. Calculated as: (Actual quantity of hours used x Standard price) - (Standard quantity of hours budgeted x Standard price).

        i. If the actual number of hours worked is greater than the standard number of hours allowed, the variance is unfavorable.

        ii. If the actual number of hours worked is less than the number of standard hours allowed, the variance is favorable.

E. Direct materials variances examine the difference between the actual and flexible budget direct materials costs.

    1. Direct materials price variance--shows whether the price incurred per unit of direct materials input was greater or less than the price expected.

        a. Usually assumed to be controllable by the purchasing department.

        b. Calculated as: (Actual price x Actual quantity purchased) - (Standard price x Actual quantity purchased).

            i. If the actual price is greater than the standard price allowed, the variance is unfavorable.

      ii.   If the actual price is less than the standard price allowed, the variance is favorable.

2.   Direct materials usage variance--indicates whether the actual quantity of direct materials used during the period was greater or less than the amount budgeted.

    a.   Assumed to be controllable by the production department.

    b.   Calculated as: (Actual quantity used x Standard price) - (Standard quantity budgeted x Standard price).

        i.   If the actual quantity of materials used is greater than the standard quantity of materials used, the variance is unfavorable.

        ii.   If the actual quantity of materials used is less than the standard quantity of materials used, the variance is favorable.

3.   Direct materials inventory variance--the difference between the quantity of direct materials purchased and the quantity used in production.

    a.   Used to monitor inventory levels when a JIT system is being used.

    b.   Calculated as: (Actual quantity purchased x Standard price) - (Actual quantity used x Standard price).

        i.   If more material was purchased than used, the variance is unfavorable.

        ii.   If more material was used than purchased, the variance is favorable.

F.   ABC overhead variance analysis investigates the differences between actual overhead costs and the planned amounts.

1.   Actual overhead may differ from planned overhead for two reasons:

    a.   Overhead costs are more (or less) than expected.

    b.   Production used more (or less) of the cost driver than expected.

2.   Overhead price variance--difference between the actual amount of overhead incurred during the period and the amount of overhead applied to production during the period.

    a.   Calculated for each individual overhead cost pool.

b. Calculated as: Actual overhead incurred for the cost pool - (Actual cost driver used x Predetermined overhead rate for the cost pool).

   i. If actual overhead incurred is greater than the overhead applied to production, the variance is unfavorable.

   ii. If actual overhead incurred is less than the overhead applied to production, the variance is favorable.

3. Overhead usage variance--shows whether the amount of overhead applied was greater (or less) than the amount budgeted.

   a. Unit-related overhead usage variance is equal to (Actual cost driver used - Standard cost driver allowed) x Predetermined unit-related overhead rate.

   b. Batch-related, product sustaining, and facility-sustaining overhead usage variances are calculated as (Actual cost driver used x Predetermined overhead rate for the cost pool) - Flexible (master) budget level of overhead cost for the cost pool.

      i. If the amount of overhead applied to production is greater than the amount of overhead in the flexible budget, the variance is unfavorable.

      ii. If the amount of overhead applied to production is less than the amount of overhead in the flexible budget, the variance is favorable.

G. General variance diagram is a useful framework for conducting variance analysis. See Exhibit 13.5.

H. When should variances be investigated? What are the criteria?

1. Most companies adopt a management-by-exception approach in which only significant variances are investigated.

2. Absolute size of the variance--large variances, either favorable or unfavorable, may require additional attention.

3. Relative size of the variance in relation to the standard cost--usually large relative variances are investigated before small relative variances.

4. Trends in variances--a variance that has steadily increased through time or that is consistently either favorable or unfavorable may justify more attention than a variance that is favorable one period and unfavorable the next.

5. Costs of investigating variances--variances that can be investigated without incurring large costs will more likely be investigated than variances costing a great deal to investigate. Benefit of investigating must be greater than the cost of investigating.

II. Other performance measures used to evaluate quality and processes.

A. To control quality, companies monitor four types of quality costs. See Exhibit 13.10.

1. Prevention cost--incurred to prevent defects from occurring in the production process.

2. Appraisal cost--incurred to detect defects in the production process.

3. Internal failure cost--incurred to correct defects in products before they are shipped to the customer.

4. External failure cost--incurred to correct defects in the products after they are shipped to the customer.

B. The customer order process is monitored by measuring throughput and delivery times.

1. Throughput time--amount of time required to convert raw materials into a finished product

a. The faster the throughput time, the quicker the production process and the smaller the raw materials and work-in-process inventories.

b. Throughput time = Storing time + Waiting time + Processing time + Inspecting Time.

c. Used to control nonvalue-added activities (activities that add cost but that are not valued by the customer or required by law). The goal is to reduce or eliminate nonvalue-added activities.

2. Delivery time--time that elapses between when the customer places an order and when the customer receives that order.

    a. Faster delivery time leads to quicker customer-response time and to smaller finished goods inventories.

    b. Delivery time = Wait time before processing + Throughput time + Travel time to the customer.

    c. Goal is to reduce delivery time while maintaining a high-quality product.

Problem I

Indicate whether the following statements are either true (T) or false (F).

_____1. Effectiveness is a condition relating to whether the goals of the company were achieved during the period.

_____2. Efficiency is measured by comparing actual outputs to expected outputs.

_____3. If the actual materials used in production exceed the standard, there will be a favorable direct materials usage variance.

_____4. If only significant variances are investigated, a company is said to have adopted a philosophy of management-by-exception.

_____5. In preparing a flexible budget, the focus is on what amount of inputs should have been used given the planned level of production.

_____6. The direct labor usage variance indicates whether workers are producing products in the amount of time allowed.

_____7. The direct materials price variance is the responsibility of the production department.

_____8. A favorable price variance will always be considered positive for the company.

_____9. It is easier to assign responsibility for overhead variances since it involves only one department.

_____10. A trend in a variance is often caused by an out-of-date standard rather than a cost that is out of control.

Problem II

Indicate the correct answer by circling the appropriate letter.

1. The cost incurred to prevent defects from occurring in the production process is referred to as _____.

    a. prevention cost
    b. appraisal cost
    c. internal failure cost
    d. external failure cost

2. A warranty cost would be an example of a/an _____.
    a. prevention cost
    b. appraisal cost
    c. internal failure cost
    d. external failure cost

3. Batch related overhead is expected to cost $2,000 per production run. During the year, X Company incurred actual overhead costs of $73,000 on its 30 production runs. X's batch related overhead price variance is _____.
   a. $13,000 favorable
   b. $13,000 unfavorable
   c. $16,500 favorable
   d. $19,000 favorable

4. Costs incurred to test products for defects are considered _____.
   a. prevention costs
   b. appraisal costs
   c. internal failure costs
   d. external failure costs

5. Y Company's unit related overhead is allocated based on direct labor hours used. The predetermined overhead rate is $9 per hour and $90,000 was charged to production during the month. Standard hours for the month's production was 11,000 hours. Based on the preceding information, Y Company's unit related usage variance was _____.
   a. $9,000 favorable
   b. $22,000 unfavorable
   c. $11,000 favorable
   d. $11,000 unfavorable

6. Disposal of defective products would be considered a/an _____.
   a. prevention cost
   b. appraisal cost
   c. internal failure cost
   d. external failure cost

Problem III

Following is a list of important ideas and key concepts from the chapter. To test your knowledge of these terms, match the term with the definition by placing the number in the space provided.

_____ Appraisal cost	_____ Process
_____ Delivery time	_____ Quality
_____ Effectiveness	_____ Standard cost
_____ Efficiency	_____ Standard price
_____ External failure cost	_____ Standard quantity
_____ Flexible budget	_____ Throughput time
_____ Internal failure cost	_____ Value-added activity
_____ Management-by-exception	_____ Variance
_____ Nonvalue-added activity	_____ Variance analysis
_____ Prevention cost	

1. The methods used to achieve the company's goals

2. The inquiry into variances to determine their causes

3. A condition relating to whether the goals of the company were achieved with the best combination of the company's resources

4. The degree of excellence in the company's products and services

5. A budget prepared based on the actual production level of the period

6. The difference between the budgeted and actual financial amounts of an input

7. The cost incurred to detect defects in the production process

8. A predetermined cost estimate of a particular operating input; calculated as the standard price times the standard quantity.

9. The cost incurred to correct defects after the product reaches the customer

10. The cost incurred to prevent defects from occurring in the production process

11. The estimated price of an input

12. A condition relating to whether the goals of the company were achieved during the period

13. The time that elapses between when the customer places an order and when he or she receives the products

14. The estimated quantity of an input expected per unit of output

15. The cost incurred to correct defects before the product reaches the customer

16. Any activity that adds value to the product or that is required by law

17. A philosophy in which only significant variances are investigated

18. The amount of time required to convert raw materials into a finished product

19. Any activity that adds cost to the product but is not valued by customers or required by law

Problem IV

Complete the following sentences by filling in the correct response.

1. If the actual price paid for materials is greater than the standard price, there will be a/an _____ materials price variance.

2. Monitoring operations involves a process of comparing the budgets developed in the _____ phase to the results of operations carried out in the _____ phase.

3. A manufacturing company compares _____ to _____ output to measure the company's effectiveness and uses _____ _____ to measure efficiency.

4. _____ is a condition relating to whether a company's goals were achieved with the best combination of resources.

5. Poor quality of direct materials may cause a/an _____ material price variance but result in a/an _____ materials usage variance.

6. If the actual direct labor hours used are less than the standard direct labor hours, there will be a/an _____ direct labor usage variance.

7. Effectiveness is measured by comparing _____ outputs of the company to _____ outputs.

8. The estimated cost of an input is determined by multiplying the _____ _____ by the _____ _____.

9. The flexible budget allows management to interpret results of operations based on _____ versus the _____ level of production.

10. The _____ department is responsible for controlling the direct materials usage variance.

11. Both _____ and _____ costs are voluntary in that a company intentionally spends money on these items in an attempt to increase quality.

12. To increase the efficiency with which orders are filled, companies monitor _____ and _____ times.

13. The direct materials inventory variance is the difference between the quantity of direct materials _____ and the quantity _____ in production, times the _____ price.

Problem V

The following information is available for Lextar manufacturing for the month of August:

10,000 board feet of lumber were purchased for $4,500
5,700 board feet were used in production
800 hours of direct labor costing $5,800 were used in production
standard quantity allowed for actual production was 6,000 board feet
standard quantity of labor allowed for production was 750 hours
standard direct labor rate is $8.00 per hour
standard price is $.40 per board foot

Calculate the following variances for the month of August:

Direct materials price variance:

Direct materials usage variance:

Direct labor price variance:

Direct labor usage variance:

Pause and Reflect:

The direct labor usage variance is assumed to be controllable by the production department. Under what circumstances might an unfavorable direct labor usage variance not be the direct result of production department activities?

_____
_____
_____
_____
_____
_____
_____
_____
_____
_____
_____
_____
_____
_____
_____
_____
_____
_____
_____

Solutions for Chapter 13

Problem 1

1. T
2. F
3. F
4. T
5. F

6. T
7. F
8. F
9. F
10. T

Problem II

1. a
2. d
3. b
4. b
5. a
6. c

Problem III

7 Appraisal cost
13 Delivery time
12 Effectiveness
3 Efficiency
9 External failure cost
5 Flexible budget
15 Internal failure cost
17 Management-by-exception
19 Nonvalue-added activity
10 Prevention cost

1 Process
4 Quality
8 Standard cost
11 Standard price
14 Standard quantity
18 Throughput time
16 Value-added activity
6 Variance
2 Variance analysis